bruno walter
erich leinsdorf
georg solti

gramophone stalwarts

3 separate discographies
compiled by john hunt

contents

5 acknowledgement

6 introduction

9 bruno walter

143 erich leinsdorf

239 georg solti

Gramophone Stalwarts
Published by John Hunt.
© 2001 John Hunt
reprinted 2009
ISBN 978-1-901395-07-5

Sole distributors:
Travis & Emery,
17 Cecil Court,
London, WC2N 4EZ,
United Kingdom.
(+44) 20 7 459 2129.
sales@travis-and-emery.com

acknowledgement

these publications have been made possible by contributions or advance subscriptions from

Stefano Angeloni
Yoshihiro Asada
Charles Brooke
George Burr
George Cobby
Dennis Davis
Richard Dennis
Hans-Peter Ebner*
Andrew Fox
Peter Fülöp
Jean-Pierre Goossens
Johann Gratz
Michael Harris
Naoya Hirabayashi
Martin Holland
Bodo Igesz
Detlef Kissmann
John Larsen
Elisabeth Legge-Schwarzkopf*
John Mallinson*
Carlo Marinelli
Bruce Morrison
Alessandro Nava
Hugh Palmer*
Laurence Pateman
Johann Christian Petersen
Yves Saillard
Robin Scott
Yoshihiko Suzuki*
Urs Weber*
G. Wright

Stathis Arfanis
E.C. Blake
Gordon Buffard
Edward Chibas*
Robert Dandois
F. De Vilder
John Derry
Henry Fogel*
Nobuo Fukumoto
Brian Godfrey
N. Goulty
A.C. Greenburgh
Tadashi Hasegawa*
Don Hodgman
Chris Hunt
Rodney Kempster
Bent Klovborg
Douglas MacIntosh
Norman MacDougall
Neil Mantle
Philip Moores
W. Moyle
Alan Newcombe
Jim Parsons*
James Pearson
Linda Perkins
Ingo Schwarz
Tom Scragg*
H.A. Van Dijk
Nigel Wood

*indicates life subscriber

Introduction

Few top-ranking conductors of the twentieth century were able to resist entirely the power of the gramophone. This applies even to Carlos Kleiber and Sergiu Celibidache, and for the latter in a most ironical way given the circumstances of his life-long aversion to the medium. The vast majority accepted it as an essential tool for spreading their fame and influence - an attitude which only seems to have become suspect in our politically correct age – or embraced it wholeheartedly as an integral part of their international careers. The present volume of conductor discographies contains examples of both philosophies.

Bruno Walter's recording career actually began in the pre-electric era, starting in 1924 with the two main orchestras of his birthplace Berlin. The work of Erich Leinsdorf and Georg Solti continued until the time of their respective deaths in the final decade of the twentieth century. What we have, in each of these three cases, is examples of musicians actually born in important European cultural centres (Berlin, Vienna and Budapest respectively) but who were compelled by prevailing political trends to seek their main careers further to the West in Europe and then mainly in the United States. Walter was of course already an established musical personality when he fled Nazi Germany and Austria, whilst Solti can be described as a comparative latecomer on the American scene, gaining prominence only with the signing of his contract to record with the Chicago Symphony Orchestra.

There is one area in which these discographies cannot claim to be complete, and that is the field of surviving recordings from live concerts and opera performances. In order to supplement the documentation which I already possess I must rely heavily on information which other enthusiasts can supply, and I am always happy to hear from them. In the case of even the most well-charted recording career the live performance recording, even if unofficial and in less than perfect sound quality, can add surprising dimensions to our knowledge of an artist's achievement.

As explained in other recent discographies I have not attempted to give Japanese catalogue numbers, unless of course they represent the sole publication of a particular item. It is by now well-known to most record collectors that in this most assiduous market for records of Western classical music, every European and American issue from both major and minor companies receives continued exposure with constant publication and republication under miriad Japanese catalogue numbers – in most cases a seemingly more thorough coverage than in the Western market of its origin.

In my continuing efforts to make the recording data as comprehensible as possible to the layman collector I will emphasise again that recording dates are as precise as can be ascertained; however where a period extends over several dates it should not be assumed that the recording of an individual work necessarily took place on every intervening day; final completion of a recording delayed until a much later date is added as a footnote at the bottom of the third (right hand) column after the various publication numbers.

Abbreviations are kept to an absolute minimum, particularly in the second (central) column where orchestras are named, followed by chorus and vocal or instrumental soloists. SO denotes Symphony Orchestra (as in NBC SO, Columbia SO, London SO and so on). Columbia Symphony Orchestra, as the name implies, was the group assembled by that American recording company and drawn mainly from members of the Metropolitan Opera Orchestra; however, for the final stereo sessions of Bruno Walter starting in 1958 a stronger contingent from the Los Angeles Philharmonic appears to have been used.

Not for the first time I gratefully acknowledge that these discographies would not have reached publication without the encouragement and the supply of much essential detail from Michael Gray and Malcolm Walker. In addition my thanks goes to Richard Chlupaty, Siam Chowkwanyun, Syd Gray, Bill Holland, Roderick Krüsemann, Robin Scott and Jerome Weber.

John Hunt January 2001

bruno walter
1876-1962

ON

COLUMBIA
RECORDS

HIS MOST RECENT RECORDINGS INCLUDE:

Symphony No. 6 — Pastorale — Beethoven
conducting the Philadelphia Orchestra
LX 963-7

Symphony No. 4 in G Major — Mahler
conducting the Philharmonic-Symphony Orchestra of New York
with Desi Halban (Soprano)
LX 949-54

Concerto No. 5 in E Flat — Beethoven
conducting the Vienna Philharmonic Orchestra
with Walter Gieseking (Pianoforte)
LX 342-6

For further recordings by this world-famous Conductor see the
Columbia Record Catalogue.

THE FINEST NAME ON RECORD

COLUMBIA GRAPHOPHONE CO. LTD., HAYES, MIDDLESEX

JOHANN SEBASTIAN BACH (1685-1750)

matthäus-passion, part one
new york	new york	lp: discocorp WSA 702-703
18 april	philharmonic	cd: phonographe PHC 5031-5032
1943	nypso choir	cd: as-disc AS 406
	conner	cd: minerva MNA 20
	watson	*discocorp and as-disc dated january 1945*
	hain	
	harrell	
	janssen	
	alvary	
	sung in english	

prelude and fugue no 4 bwv 849/wohltemperiertes klavier
los angeles	walter, piano	cd: wing (japan) WCD 51
2 july		
1952		

SAMUEL BARBER (1910-1981)

symphony no 1
new york	new york	78: columbia LX 1077-1078
23 january	philharmonic	78: columbia (usa) X 252
1945		cd: sony SMK 64466/SX10K 66247
		cd: pearl GEM 0049
		cd: magic talent CD 48014
		cd: history 205246/205241

LUDWIG VAN BEETHOVEN (1770-1827)

symphony no 1

new york 25 march 1939	nbc so	cd: eklipse (japan) T 4

new york 29 november 1947	new york philharmonic	78: columbia LX 1204-1207 78: columbia (italy) GQX 11313-11316 78: columbia (usa) M 796 lp: columbia (france) 33FC 1005 lp: columbia (usa) ML 2027/ML 4790 lp: philips ABL 3239/A09400L/ GBL 5615/G03593L lp: cbs 77511 cd: dante LYS 397 cd: grammofono AB 78805-78806 cd: theorema THS 121143

los angeles 1951	los angeles philharmonic	unpublished radio broadcast

los angeles
5 january
1959
	columbia so	lp: columbia (usa) ML 5398/MS 6078/
		    D7L-265/D7S-610/Y7-30051
		lp: philips ABL 3346/SABL 168/
		    A01473L/835 540AY
		lp: cbs BRG 72056/SBRG 72056
		cd: sony MK 42009/MYK 44775/
		    SMK 64460/SX6K 48099

beethoven **symphony no 2**
new york   new york   lp: columbia (usa) ML 4596
17 march   philharmonic   lp: philips ABL 3240/A09401L/
1952   GBL 5615/G03593L
                                     lp: cbs 77511

los angeles   columbia so   lp: columbia (usa) ML 5398/MS 6078/
9 january   D7L-265/D7S-610/Y7-30051/
1959   YT 35940
                                     lp: philips ABL 3346/SABL 168/
                                          A01473L/835 540AY
                                     lp: cbs BRG 72056/SBRG 72056
                                     cd: sony MK 42009/MYK 44775/
                                          SMK 64460/SX6K 48099

beethoven **symphony no 3 "eroica"**

new york 20 january 1941	new york philharmonic	78: columbia (usa) M 449 cd: dante LYS 308-309 cd: grammofono AB 78838-78839 cd: history 205243/205241
new york 21 march 1949	new york philharmonic	78: columbia (usa) M 858 lp: columbia 33CX 1117 lp: columbia (france) 33FCX 232 lp: columbia (italy) 33QCX 10061 lp: columbia (usa) ML 4228/A 1072 lp: philips ABL 3241/A09402L/ GBL 5617G03594L lp: cbs 77511 cd: theorema THS 121143
new york 3 february 1957	symphony of the air	lp: replica RPL 2472 lp: cls records CLS 2054 lp: discocorp BWS 1010 lp: movimento musica 08.001 cd: music and arts CD 4010 *recorded at toscanini memorial concert*

los angeles
20-25
january
1958
	columbia so	lp: columbia (usa) ML 5320/MS 6036/
		    D7L-265/D7S-610/Y7-30051/
		    Y 33925
		lp: philips ABL 3347/SABL 132/
		    A01449L/835 507AY
		lp: cbs BRG 72057/SBRG 72057
		cd: sony MK 42010/MYK 42599/
		    SMK 64461/SX6K 48099

beethoven **symphony no 4**
new york   new york   lp: columbia (usa) ML 4596
24 march   philharmonic   lp: philips ABL 3249/A09401L/
1952   GBL 5616/G03593L/G05627R
                                  lp: cbs 77511

los angeles   columbia so   lp: columbia (usa) ML 5365/MS 6055/
8-10   D7L-265/D7S-610/Y7-30051/
february   Y 30314
1958   lp: philips ABL 3348/SABL 167/
                                      A01474L/835 541AY
                                  lp: cbs BRG 72058/SBRG 72058
                                  cd: sony MK 42011/SMK 64462/
                                      SX6K 48099

symphony no 4, rehearsal of second movement
los angeles   columbia so   lp: columbia (usa) and philips
february   *lp only available when complete symphonies*
1958   *purchased as a boxed set*

beethoven **symphony no 5**

london 19-22 november 1926	orchestra of the royal philharmonic society	columbia unpublished

new york february 1942	new york philharmonic	78: columbia (usa) M 498 78: columbia (switzerland) LZX 207-210 lp: columbia (usa) ML 4009 cd: dante LYS 308-309 *dante dated 15 december 1941*

new york
13 february
1950
	new york
	philharmonic
		lp: columbia 33CX 1077
		lp: columbia (usa) ML 4297/
		    ML 4790/CL 918
		lp: philips ABL 3239/A09400L/
		    GBL 5615/G03593L
		lp: cbs 77511

los angeles
27-30
january
1958
	columbia so	lp: columbia (usa) ML 5365/MS 6055/
		    D7L-265/DS7-610/Y7-30051/
		    Y 30314
		lp: philips ABL 2238/SABL 167/
		    A01474L/835 541AY/610 300VR
		lp: cbs BRG 72058/SBRG 72058
		cd: sony MK 42011/SMK 64463/
		    SX6K 48099
		rehearsal extracts
		lp: columbia (usa) MS 6506

beethoven **symphony no 6 "pastoral"**

vienna 5-18 december 1936	vienna philharmonic	78: hmv DB 3051-3055/ 　　DB 8219-8223 auto 78: victor M 272/G 20 lp: hmv (italy) QRX 9016/QIM 6301 lp: turnabout THS 65042 lp: emi 1C147 50149-50151M cd: preiser 90157 cd: avid AMSC 583 cd: dante LYS 518-519 *also private lp edition by preiser*
philadelphia 10-12 january 1946	philadelphia orchestra	78: columbia LX 963-967 78: columbia (italy) 　　GQX 11308-11312 78: columbia (usa) M 631 lp: columbia (usa) ML 4010/A 1062 lp: columbia (france) 33FCX 144 lp: columbia (italy) 33QCX 144 lp: philips GBL 5618/G03595L/G05642R lp: cbs 77511 cd: grammofono AB 78805-78806 cd: history 204553-308
los angeles 1951	los angeles philharmonic	unpublished radio broadcast
los angeles 13-17 january 1958	columbia so	lp: columbia (usa) ML 5284/MS 6012/ 　　D7L-265/D7S-610/Y7-30051 lp: philips ABL 3349/SABL 133/ 　　A01475L/835 501AY lp: cbs BRG 72059/SBRG 72059/ 　　MY 36720 cd: sony MK 42012/MYK 36720/ 　　MYK 42536/SMK 64462/ 　　SX6K 48099

beethoven **symphony no 7**

new york 12 march 1951	new york philharmonic	lp: columbia 33CX 1120 lp: columbia (usa) ML 4414 lp: philips ABL 3243/A09404L/ GBL 5619/G03596L lp: cbs 77511 cd: palladio PD 4163 cd: historical performers HP 15

los angeles
1-12
february
1958
	columbia so	lp: columbia (usa) ML 5404/MS 6082/
		     D7L-265/D7S-610/Y7-30051/
		     Y 30314/YT 35219/KLC 2700
		lp: philips ABL 3350/SABL 166/
		     A01476L/835 529AY
		lp: cbs BRG 72060/SBRG 72060
		cd: sony MK 42013/MYK 44829/
		     SMK 64463/SX6K 48099

symphony no 7, rehearsal of first movement

los angeles february 1958	columbia so	lp: columbia (usa) and philips *lp only available when complete symphonies* *purchased as a boxed set*

symphony no 8

new york
18 april
1942
	new york
	philharmonic
		78: columbia (usa) M 525
		lp: columbia (usa) ML 2001/SL 186
		lp: philips ABL 3243/A09404L/
		     GBL 5619/G03596L/A01602R/
		     S06625R
		lp: cbs 77511
		cd: phonographe PHC 5028
		cd: dante LYS 308-309
		cd: grammofono AB 78805-78806
		cd: history 205243/205241

los angeles
6-17
january
and 12
february
1958
	columbia so	lp: columbia (usa) M2L-264/M2S-608/
		     D7L-265/D7S-610/Y7-30051/
		     Y 30314/YT 35219
		lp: philips ABL 3351/SABL 169/
		     A01477L/835 542AY
		lp: cbs BRG 72061/SBRG 72061
		cd: sony MK 42013/MYK 44829/
		     SMK 64461/SX6K 48099

beethoven **symphony no 9 "choral"**

london 13 november 1947	london philharmonic orchestra and chorus baillie ferrier nash parsons	lp: discocorp BWS 742 cd: music and arts CD 733/CD 4733
new york 16 april- 4 may 1949	new york philharmonic westminster choir gonsalez nikolaidi jobin harrell	78: columbia (usa) M 900 lp: columbia (usa) SL 56/SL 156 lp: columbia (france) 33FCX 113-114 lp: columbia (italy) 33QCX 113-114 lp: philips A01304L-A01305L

new york
9 march
1953
	new york
	philharmonic
	westminster
	choir
	yeend
	lipton
	lloyd
	harrell
		lp: columbia (usa) SL 186/ML 5200/
		    A 1067/3216 0322
		lp: philips ABL 3243-3244/
		    A09404L-A09405L/GBL 5620/
		    G03598L
		lp: cbs 61728/72322/77511
		cd: sony MPK 45552
		this was a remake of final choral movement only: first three movements were taken from the 1949 performance listed above

vienna 13 november 1955	vienna philharmonic vienna opera chorus güden höngen majkut frick	cd: nuova era NE 2249 *performance during celebrations to re-open vienna staatsoper*

beethoven symphony no 9/concluded

los angeles	columbia so	lp:	columbia (usa) M2L-264/M2S-608/ D7L-265/D7S-610/MP 39029/Y7-30051
19-31	westminster		
january	choir	lp:	philips ABL 3351-3352/ SABL 169-170/A01477L-A01478L/ 835 542AY-835 543AY
1959	cundari		
	rankin		
	de costa	lp:	cbs BRG 72061-72062/ SBRG 72061-72062/60506/ 61011-61012/61233
	wildermann		
		lp:	melodiya D 028225-028228
		cd:	sony MK 42014/SMK 64464/ SX6K 48099

choral movement recorded in new york between 6-15 april 1959

symphony no 9, rehearsal of second movement
los angeles   columbia so   lp: columbia (usa) and philips
january   *lp only available when complete symphonies*
1959   *purchased as a box set*

missa solemnis
new york   new york   cd: as-disc AS 301
18 april   philharmonic   cd: iron needle IN 1418
1948   westminster   cd: urania URN 22135
              choir   *also issued in japan by discocorp*
              steber
              merriman
              hain
              alvary

beethoven **piano concerto no 5 "emperor"**

vienna	vienna	78: columbia LX 342-346
10-11	philharmonic	78: columbia (germany) LWX 83-87
october	gieseking	78: columbia (france) LFX 359-363
1934		78: columbia (italy) GQX 10764-10768
		78: columbia (usa) M 243
		lp: turnabout THS 65011
		lp: rococo 2019
		lp: emi 3C153 52700-52705M/
		1C147 50149-50151M/153 52700
		cd: grammofono AB 78506
		cd: dante LYS 518-519
		cd: radio years RY 61
		cd: appian APR 5512
		appian dated september 1934
new york	new york	78: columbia (usa) M 500
22 december	philharmonic	78: columbia (switzerland)
1941	serkin	LZX 222-226
		lp: columbia (usa) ML 4004
		lp: columbia (japan) SOC 127
		cd: sony SMK 64487/SX9K 66249
		cd: dante LYS 308-309
		cd: historic performers HP 15
		cd: palladio PD 4163
		cd: biddulph LHW 026

schwann catalogue states that a performance of piano concerto no 4 with serkin/nypo/walter also appears on historic performers cd HP 15, but this could not be verified

triple concerto

new york	new york	78: columbia (usa) M 842
21 march	philharmonic	lp: columbia (usa) ML 2029/ML 5368
1949	corigliano	lp: columbia (france) 33FC 1002
	rose	lp: columbia (italy) 33QC 1002
	hendl	lp: philips G05647R
		cd: sony SMK 64479

22
beethoven **violin concerto**

london	british so	78: columbia LX 174-178
18 april	szigeti	78: columbia (australia) LOX 157-161
1932		78: columbia (usa) M 177
		lp: emi HQM 1224
		cd: dante LYS 084
		cd: iron needle IN 1302
		cd: pearl GEMMCD 9345
		cd: music and arts CD 813

new york	new york	78: columbia LX 1298-1302
5 april	philharmonic	78: columbia (usa) M 697
1947	szigeti	lp: columbia (usa) ML 4012
		cd: sony MPK 52536/SMK 64459
		cd: dante LYS 518-519

new york	new york	cd: as-disc AS 423
15 february	philharmonic	cd: legends LGD 114
1953	wicks	

los angeles	columbia so	lp: columbia (usa) ML 5663/MS 6263/
23-26	franccscatti	Y 30042
january		lp: cbs BRG 72006/SBRG 72006
1961		cd: sony MK 42018/MBK 45637/
		SBK 47659

beethoven **fidelio**

new york	metropolitan	lp: ed smith EJS 126
22 february	opera orchestra	lp: discocorp WSA 712-713
1941	and chorus	lp: metropolitan opera MET 5
	flagstad	cd: arkadia CDHP 628/GA 2022
	farell	cd: nuova era NE 2345-2346
	maison	cd: dante LYS 023-024
	laufkötter	*excerpts*
	huehn	cd: memories HR 4456-4457
	kipnis	*spoken dialogue is replaced in this*
	janssen	*performance by recitative composed by bodansky*

new york	metropolitan	unpublished met broadcast
17 march	opera orchestra	*excerpts*
1945	and chorus	cd: walhall WHL 29
	resnik	cd: wing (japan) WCD 105-106
	greer	
	carron	
	alvary	
	garris	
	schon	
	thompson	
	sung in english	

new york	metropolitan	lp: discocorp BWS 804
10 march	opera orchestra	lp: raritas 402
1951	and chorus	
	flagstad	
	connor	
	svanholm	
	klein	
	schöffler	
	ernster	
	hines	

24
beethoven **fidelio overture**

london	bbc so	78: hmv DB 2261
21 may		78: victor 11809
1934		cd: iron needle IN 1302
		cd: dante LYS 518-519
		cd: grammofono AB 78560

leonore no 2 overture

new york	new york	cd: wing (japan) WCD 55
17 march	philharmonic	
1946		
los angeles	columbia so	lp: columbia (usa) ML 5887/MS 6487/
1 july		MY 36720/D7L-265/D7S-610/
1960		Y7-30051
		lp: cbs BRG 72155/SBRG 72155
		cd: sony MK 42012/SX6K 48099/
		SMK 64488/SX9K 66249

leonore no 3 overture

vienna	vienna	78: hmv DB 2885-2886
21 may	philharmonic	78: victor M 359
1936		cd: preiser 90157
		cd: koch 3-7011-2
		cd: grammofono AB 78517
		cd: phonographe PHC 5031-5032
		cd: dante LYS 518-519
		cd: monopoly GI 1000
		also private lp edition by preiser
new york	new york	unpublished radio broadcast
26 may	philharmonic	
1946		
new york	new york	lp: columbia (usa) ML 5232/ML 5368
4 december	philharmonic	lp: philips ABL 3225/A01367L
1954		lp: cbs DP 1
		cd: sony SMK 64487
		DP 1 incorrectly describes orchestra as columbia so

beethoven **coriolan overture**
berlin
august or
october
1923

berlin
philharmonic

78: grammophon 65928/69587
lp: dg 2740 259
cd: wing (japan) WCD 29
cd: istituto discocraphigo italiano
    IDIS 295-296

london
12 september
1938

london
symphony

78: hmv DB 3638
78: victor 12535
cd: iron needle IN 1302
cd: grammofono AB 78548
cd: dante LYS 518-519

los angeles
15 april
1959

columbia so

lp: columbia (usa) ML 5887/MS 6487/
    D7L-265/D7S-610/Y7-30051
lp: cbs BRG 72155/SBRG 72155/GS 6
cd: sony MK 42010/MYK 42599/
    SX6K 48099/SMK 64460

egmont overture
new york
11 november
1943

new york
philharmonic

cd: wing (japan) WCD 16

berlin
25 september
1950

berlin
philharmonic

lp: discocorp BWS 726/BWS 1010
cd: arkadia CDGI 738

new york
4 december
1954

new york
philharmonic

lp: columbia (usa) ML 5232
lp: philips ABL 3225/A01367L/G03520L
lp: cbs DP 1
cd: sony SMK 64488
*DP1 incorrectly describes orchestra as
columbia so*

beethoven **die geschöpfe des prometheus overture**
london british so 78: columbia LX 277
1930 78: columbia (usa) 68091D

boston boston cd: wing (japan) WCD 58
21 january symphony
1947

new york new york unpublished radio broadcast
20 december philharmonic
1953

lieder: wonne der wehmut; mit einem gemalten band
washington schumann lp: voce VOCE 117
2 april walter, piano lp: columbia (japan) OW 7225
1950 cd: wing (japan) WCD 51

HECTOR BERLIOZ (1803-1869)

symphonie fantastique
paris	paris	78: hmv DB 3852-3857
19-20	conservatoire	78: victor M 662
may	orchestra	lp: victor CAL 281
1939		lp: rococo 2016
		lp: emi 3C051 03611
		cd: grammofono AB 78580
		cd: iron needle IN 1305
		cd: vai audio VAIA 1081
		cd: history 205243/205241
new york	new york	cd: cetra CDE 1006/CDE 3021
18-21	philharmonic	cd: music and arts CD 822/CD 4822
november		cd: nuova era NE 2392
1954		cd: palladio PD 4202

benvenuto cellini overture
berlin	staatskapelle	78: grammophon 66075-66076
1924		

le carnaval romain overture
berlin	berlin	78: grammophon 65929/69588
august or	philharmonic	cd: wing (japan) WCD 29
october		
1923		

le corsaire overture
new york	nbc so	cd: as-disc AS 414
1 april		cd: music and arts CD 248/CD 4273
1939		

EDINBURGH
INTERNATIONAL FESTIVAL
of
MUSIC and DRAMA

IN ASSOCIATION WITH THE ARTS COUNCIL OF GREAT BRITAIN
AND THE CORPORATION OF THE CITY OF EDINBURGH

USHER HALL

Vienna Philharmonic Orchestra

Conductor   BRUNO WALTER

Soloists
KATHLEEN FERRIER   PETER PEARS

Thursday, 11th September 1947, at 7.30 p.m.

Friday, 12th September 1947, at 2.30 p.m.

berlioz menuet des follets/la damnation de faust

new york 1 april 1939	nbc so	cd: as-disc AS 414 cd: music and arts CD 248/CD 4273
los angeles 21 may 1950	los angeles philharmonic	cd: eklipse EKR 1402 cd: nuova era NE 2392 *nuova era incorrectly describes* *orchestra as new york philharmonic*

ballet des sylphes/la damnation de faust

london 5 december 1924	orchestra of the royal philharmonic society	78: columbia L 1623 cd: iron needle IN 1305
london 19 november 1925	orchestra of the royal philharmonic society	78: columbia (usa) M 15
new york 1 april 1939	nbc so	cd: as-disc AS 414 cd: music and arts CD 248/CD 4273
los angeles 21 may 1950	los angeles philharmonic	cd: eklipse EKR 1402 cd: nuova era NE 2392 *nuova era incorrectly describes* *orchestra as new york philharmonic*

marche hongroise/la damnation de faust

new york 1 april 1939	nbc so	cd: as-disc AS 414 cd: music and arts CD 248/CD 4273
los angeles 21 may 1950	los angeles philharmonic	cd: eklipse EKR 1402 cd: nuova era NE 2392 *nuova era incorrectly describes* *orchestra as new york philharmonic*

GEORGES BIZET (1838-1875)

carmen, fragmentary excerpts
vienna 22-27 december 1937	vienna philharmonic vienna opera chorus brems rethy mazaroff arnold pierotic monthy *sung in german*	cd: koch 3-1450-2/3-1456-2

carmen, act three entr'acte
berlin august or october 1923	berlin philharmonic	78: grammophon 65954/65956

carmen, act four entr'acte
berlin august or october 1923	berlin philharmonic	78: grammophon 65954

ERNEST BLOCH (1880-1959)

evocations suite
new york february 1941	new york philharmonic	cd: as-disc AS 421 *urania cd catalogue incorrectly states that* *this performance is contained on URN 22141*

JOHANNES BRAHMS (1833-1897)

symphony no 1

vienna 3-5 may 1937	vienna philharmonic	78: hmv DB 3277-3281 78: victor M 470 lp: emi 1C047 01655 lp: discocorp BWS 803 cd: preiser 90114 cd: avid AMSC 603 cd: grammofono AB 78517 cd: history 205244/205241
los angeles 7 october 1947	los angeles philharmonic	cd: eklipse (japan) T 5
new york 30 december 1953	new york philharmonic	lp: columbia (usa) ML 5124/SL 200/ 3236 0007 lp: philips ABR 4037/A01625R/ GBL 5603
los angeles 25 november 1959	columbia so	lp: columbia (usa) ML 5789/MS 6389/ Y-30311/M4L-252/D4S-615 lp: philips ABL 3341/SABL 181 lp: cbs BRG 72088/SBRG 72088/ 72087 cd: sony MK 42020/MYK 44827/ SMK 64470

brahms **symphony no 2**

new york 24 february 1940	nbc so	unpublished radio broadcast
philadelphia 12 february 1944	philadelphia orchestra	cd: wing (japan) WCD 49
berlin 25 september 1950	berlin philharmonic	cd: arkadia CDGI 738 cd: legends LGD 148 cd: music and arts CD 239 cd: urania awaiting publication

new york
28-30
december
1953
	new york
	philharmonic
		lp: columbia (usa) ML 5125/SL 200/
		    3236 0007
		lp: philips ABL 3095/A01163L/
		    GBL 5604
		cd: theorema THS 121213
		rehearsal extract
		lp: columbia (usa) 32785

paris 5 may 1955	orchestre national	lp: discocorp BWS 803 cd: nuova era NE 2226
vancouver 1958	vanvouver international festival orchestra	vhs video: vai audio VAI 69407 *rehearsal extracts* vhs video: vai audio VAI 69047 vhs video: teldec 4509 950386 laserdisc: teldec 4509 950386

los angeles
11-16
january
1960
	columbia so	lp: columbia (usa) ML 5573/MS 6173/
		    M4L-252/D4S-615
		lp: philips ABL 3342/SABL 182
		lp: cbs BRG 72089/SBRG 72089/
		    72087/72330/61218/61428
		cd: sony MK 42021/MYK 44870/
		    SMK 64471

brahms **symphony no 3**
vienna   vienna   78: hmv DB 2933-2936/
18-21   philharmonic   DB 8169-8172 auto
may   78: victor M 341
1936   lp: hmv (italy) QIM 6341
                                      lp: discocorp BWS 803
                                      cd: koch 3-7120-2
                                      also private lp edition by preiser

new york   new york   lp: columbia (usa) ML 5126/ML 4927/
21-23   philharmonic   SL 200/3236 0007
december   lp: philips ABR 4031/A01623R/
1953   GBL 5605
                                      rehearsal extract
                                      lp: columbia (usa) 32785

los angeles   columbia so   lp: columbia (usa) ML 5574/MS 6174/
27-30   M4L-252/D4S-615
january   lp: philips ABL 3343/SABL 183/
1960   A01464L/835 557AY
                                      lp: cbs BRG 72090/SBRG 72090/
                                          72087/72331/61219
                                      cd: sony MK 42022/MYK 42531/
                                          SMK 64471

34
brahms **symphony no 4**

london	bbc so	78: hmv DB 2253-2257
21 may		78: victor M 242
1934		78: columbia (japan) J 8005-8009
		lp: victor CAL 246
		lp: bbc records BBC 4001
		lp: discocorp BWS 803
		cd: koch 3-7120-2
		cd: grammofono AB 78560
new york	new york	cd: nuova era NE 2303
10 march	philharmonic	cd: wing (japan) WCD 33
1946		*nuova era incorrectly describes*
		orchestra as vienna philharmonic
new york	new york	lp: columbia (usa) ML 5127/ML 4472/
21 february	philharmonic	SL 200/3236 007/A 1090
1951		lp: philips ABL 3008/A01118L/
		GBL 5606
los angeles	columbia so	lp: columbia (usa) ML 5439/MS 6113/
4-14		M4L-252/D4S-615/Y-32373
february		lp: philips ABL 3342/SABL 184
1959		lp: cbs BRG 72091/SBRG 72091/
		72087/61211
		cd: sony MK 42023/MYK 44776/
		SMK 64472

brahms **piano concerto no 1**
amsterdam	concertgebouw	lp: discocorp IGI 728
20 february	orchestra	cd: legends LGD 105
1936	horowitz	cd: as-disc AS 400
		cd: music and arts CD 810
		cd: radio years RY 54

section from first movement missing: replaced with section from performance with horowitz conducted by toscanini

new york	new york	unpublished radio broadcast
4 february	philharmonic	
1951	curzon	

piano concerto no 2
new york	new york	lp: discocorp BWS 736
11 february	philharmonic	cd: as-disc AS 415
1951	hess	cd: music and arts CD 779

violin concerto
new york	new york	unpublished radio broadcast
18-21	philharmonic	
january	francescatti	
1951		

new york	new york	lp: discocorp (japan) BWS 1025
20 december	philharmonic	cd: wing (japan) WCD 36
1953	morini	

1937 performance of the concerto with huberman and new york philharmonic issued on wing (japan) WCD 33 may not be conducted by walter

brahms **double concerto**

new york 1-4 january 1951	new york philharmonic corigliano rose	cd: nuova era NE 2226
new york 29 november 1954	new york philharmonic stern rose	lp: columbia (usa) ML 5076 lp: philips ABL 3139/A01244L/ GBL 5614/G05628R cd: sony SM3K 45952

los angeles
20 november
1959
	columbia so
	francescatti
	fournier
		lp: columbia (usa) ML 5493/MS 6158
		lp: philips ABL 3343/SABL 185/
		    A01466L
		lp: cbs BRG 72087/SBRG 72087
		cd: sony MK 42024/MYK 44771/
		    SMK 64479

hungarian dance no 1

new york
12 february
1951
	new york
	philharmonic
		45: philips ABE 10002/A409 056E/
		    N409513E
		lp: columbia (usa) ML 4908/ML 5126/
		    AAL 1/SL 200/3236 0007
		lp: philips G03520L
		cd: sony SMK 64467

brahms **hungarian dance no 3**
new york	new york	45: philips ABE 10002/A409056E/N409513E
12 february	philharmonic	lp: columbia (usa) ML 4908/ML 5126/
1951		AAL 1/SL 200/3236 007/DP 1
		cd: sony SMK 64467
		DP 1 incorrectly describes orchestra as columbia so

hungarian dance no 10
new york	new york	45: philips ABE 10002/A409056E/N409513E
12 february	philharmonic	lp: columbia (usa) ML 4908/ML 5126/
1951		AAL 1/SL 200/3236 007
		cd: sony SMK 64467

hungarian dance no 17
new york	new york	45: philips ABE 10002/A409056E/N409513E
12 february	philharmonic	lp: columbia (usa) ML 4908/ML 5126/
1951		AAL 1/SL 200/3236 007
		cd: sony SMK 64467
new york	new york	cd: wing (japan) WCD 33
16 march	philharmonic	
1953		

alto rhapsody
new york	new york	cd: wing (japan) WCD 54
9 november	philharmonic	
1941	szantho	
	westminster	
	choir	
los angeles	columbia so	lp: columbia (usa) ML 5888/MS 6488
11 january	occidental	lp: cbs BRG 72142/SBRG 72142/
1961	college choir	61428
	miller	cd: sony MK 42025/MYK 45503/
		SMK 64469

38
brahms **schicksalslied**

new york	new york	lp: columbia (usa) SL 156
15 december	philharmonic	lp: columbia (france) 33FCX 113-114
1941	westminster choir	lp: columbia (italy) 33QCX 113-114
los angeles	los angeles	cd: as-disc AS 415
7 october	philharmonic	cd: eklipse (japan) T 5
1947	strelitzer choir	cd: urania awaiting publication
rome	rai roma	lp: cetra LAR 7
16 april	orchestra	cd: cetra ARCD 2030
1952	and chorus	cd: wing (japan) WCD 57
	sung in italian	
los angeles	columbia so	lp: columbia (usa) ML 5888/MS 6488
9 january	occidental	lp: cbs BRG 72142/SBRG 72142/ 61428
1961	college choir	cd: sony MK 42025/MYK 45503/ SMK 64472

wiegenlied

new york	lehmann	cd: eklipse EKR 47
12 february	walter, piano	
1950		
san francisco	lehmann	lp: discocorp BWS 807/BWS 1009
17 april	walter, piano	
1950		

lieder: immer leiser wird mein schlummer; der tod das ist die kühle nacht; botschaft; von ewiger liebe

edinburgh	ferrier	lp: discocorp BWS 707
7 september	walter, piano	lp: decca 6BB 197-198/414 6111
1949		cd: decca 414 6112/433 4762/433 8022

brahms ein deutsches requiem

london 1 november 1947	bbc so bbc chorus suddaby williams	unpublished radio broadcast *music performance research centre*
stockholm 13 september 1950	stockholm philharmonic orchestra and chorus lindberg-torlind berglund	lp: discocorp
new york 16 march 1952	new york philharmonic orchestra westminster choir conner harrell	lp: discocorp BWS 204
rome 16 april 1952	rai roma orchestra and chorus carteri christoff *sung in italian*	lp: cetra LAR 7 lp: cls records CLS 22016 cd: cetra CDAR 2029
edinburgh 8-10 september 1953	vienna philharmonic orchestra edinburgh choral union seefried fischer-dieskau	cd: wing (japan) WCD 3-4
new york 16-29 december 1954	new york philharmonic orchestra westminster choir seefried london	lp: columbia (usa) ML 4980/Y 31015/ M3P 39651 lp: cbs 61284 lp: movimento musica 02.022 cd: melodram MEL 18004 cd: sony MPK 45687/SMK 64469

40
brahms **academic festival overture**

vienna 18 october 1937	vienna philharmonic	78: hmv DB 3394 78: victor 12190 lp: victor CAL 242 lp: emi 1C047 01655 cd: avid AMSC 603 cd: urania awaiting publication
los angeles 7 october 1947	los angeles philharmonic	cd: eklipse (japan) T 5

new york
12 march
1951
	new york
	philharmonic
		lp: columbia (usa) ML 4908/
		    ML 5126/ML 5232/SL 200/
		    AAL 1/3236 0007
		lp: philips ABL 3139/ABL 3225/
		    A01244L/A01367L/
		    GBL 5614
		cd: theorema THS 121213

los angeles
16 january
1960
	columbia so	lp: columbia (usa) ML 5573/
		    ML 5761/ML 5887/MS 6178/
		    MS 6361/MS 6487/M4L-252/
		    D4S-615/Y-30851/DP 1
		lp: philips ABL 3342/SABL 182
		lp: cbs BRG 72089/BRG 72097/
		    BRG 72155/SBRG 72089/
		    SBRG 72097/SBRG 72155/
		    61211
		cd: sony MK 42021/MYK 44870/
		    SMK 64470

brahms **tragic overture**

london 18 january 1939	bbc so	unpublished radio broadcast *music performance research centre*
philadelphia 12 february 1944	philadelphia orchestra	cd: wing (japan) WCD 49
edinburgh 8 september 1953	vienna philharmonic	cd: wing (japan) WCD 3-4
new york 18-23 september 1953	new york philharmonic	lp: columbia (usa) ML 4814/ ML 4908/ML 4927/ML 5076/ ML 5232/SL 200/3236 0007 lp: philips ABL 3139/ABL 3225/ A01244L/A01367L/GBL 5614 cd: theorema THS 121213
los angeles 23 january 1960	columbia so	lp: columbia (usa) ML 5493/ ML 5573/MS 6158/MS 6173/ M4L-252/D4S-615/Y-30851 lp: philips ABL 3343/SABL 183/ A01464L/835 557AY lp: cbs BRG 72090/SBRG 72090/ 72330/61218 cd: sony MK 42023/MYK 44776/ SMK 64472

brahms **haydn variations**

los angeles 7 october 1947	los angeles philharmonic	cd: eklipse (japan) T 5

new york   new york   45: philips ABE 10056/A409 071E
18-19   philharmonic   lp: columbia (usa) ML 4814/ML 4911/
september   ML 4927/ML 5076/SL 200/
1953   3236 0007
                                     lp: philips ABL 3095/ABL 3139/
                                         A01163L/G03520L
                                     cd: sony MHK 63328

los angeles   columbia so   lp: columbia (usa) ML 5493/ML 5574/
18-30   MS 6158/MS 6174/M4L-252/
january   D4S-615/Y-30851
1960   lp: philips ABL 3343/SABL 185/
                                         A01466L/835 559AY
                                     lp: cbs BRG 72087/SBRG 72087/
                                         60298/61219
                                     cd: sony MK 42022/MYK 42531/
                                         SMK 64470

ANTON BRUCKNER (1824-1896)

symphony no 4 "romantic"

new york 10 february 1940	nbc so	cd: eklipse (japan) T 4 cd: pearl GEMMCD 9131 cd: history 205245/205241 *history dated 2 march 1940*
los angeles 13-17 february 1960	columbia so	lp: columbia (usa) M2L-273/M2S-622/R44X lp: cbs BRG 72011-72012/ SBRG 72011-72012/ 60297/61137 cd: sony MK 42035/MBK 44825/ MYK 44871/SMK 64481

symphony no 7

los angeles 11-23 march 1961	columbia so	lp: columbia (usa) M2L-290/M2S-690/R44X Y2-35238 lp: cbs BRG 72139-72140/ SBRG 72139-72140/61128-61129 cd: sony MK 42036/M2YK 45669/ SMK 64482

symphony no 8

new york 26 january 1941	new york philharmonic	lp: discocorp BWS 808 cd: iron needle IN 1353-1354 cd: historical performers HP 23

44
bruckner **symphony no 9**

new york 17 march 1946	new york philharmonic	cd: wing (japan) WCD 55
salzburg 19 august 1953	vienna philharmonic	lp: movimento musica 01.053
new york 27 december 1953	new york philharmonic	cd: nuova era NE 2225 cd: palladio PD 4209

los angeles
16-18
november
1959
	columbia so	lp: columbia (usa) ML 5571/
		    MS 6171/Y-35220/R44X
		lp: philips SABL 179/835 561AY
		lp: cbs BRG 72095/SBRG 72095/
		    61194
		cd: sony MK 42037/MBK 44825/
		    MYK 44825/SMK 64483

bruckner **te deum**
paris 29 june 1937	vienna philharmonic vienna opera chorus schumann thorborg dermota kipnis	issued on a promtional cd only in japan by toshiba
new york 7 march 1953	new york philhrmonic westminster choir yeend lipton lloyd harrell	lp: columbia (usa) ML 4980 lp: philips ABL 3189/L09408L/GBL 5629 lp: cbs 72317 cd: sony SMK 64480/SX10K 66248
vienna 13 november 1955	vienna philharmonic vienna opera chorus güden höngen majkut frick	cd: nuova era NE 2303 *performance during celebrations to* *re-open vienna staatsoper*

FERRUCCIO BUSONI (1866-1924)

violin concerto
amsterdam	concertgebouw	lp: discocorp BWS 335
12 march	orchestra	lp: rococo 2023
1936	busch	cd: music and arts CD 861/CD 4861
		cd: istituto discographico italiano IDIS 334

LUIGI CHERUBINI (1760-1842)

les deux journées, overture
berlin	staatskapelle	78: grammophon 66073
1924		

FREDERIC CHOPIN (1810-1949)

piano concerto no 1
new york	new york	lp: discocorp BWS 740
9 february	philharmonic	lp: melodram MEL 304
1947	rubinstein	cd: as-disc AS 401
		cd: historical performers HPS 29
		cd: new york philharmonic NYP 9701
		excerpt
		cd: new york philharmonic NYP 9712

nocturne op 9 no 2; valse op 62 no 2
los angeles	walter, piano	lp: discocorp BWS 807
2 july		cd: wing (japan) WCD 51
1952		

ARCANGELO CORELLI (1653-1713)

christmas concerto op 6 no 8
london	london so	78: hmv DB 3639-3640
13 september		78: victor M 600
1938		lp: discocorp WSA 702-703
boston	boston so	cd: wing (japan) WCD 57
21 january		
1947		

CLAUDE DEBUSSY (1862-1918)

la mer
new york	new york	lp: discocorp BWS 808
19 january	philharmonic	cd: as-disc AS 418
1941		

prélude a l'apres-midi d'un faune
philadelphia	philadelphia	private lp issue by philadelphia
1 march	orchestra	orchestra
1947		
los angeles	los angeles	cd: as-disc AS 418
19 june	philharmonic	
1949		

VINCENT D'INDY (1851-1931)

istar variations
new york	nbc so	unpublished radio broadcast
24 february		
1940		

ANTONIN DVORAK (1841-1904)

symphony no 8

new york 28 november 1947	new york philharmonic	78: columbia (usa) M 770 78: columbia (italy) GQX 11465-11468 lp: columbia 33CX 1036 lp: columbia (italy) 33QCX 10011 lp: columbia (usa) ML 4119 lp: philips ABL 3288/A01433L
new york 15 february 1948	new york philharmonic	cd: dante LYS 411 cd: music and arts CD 714/CD 4714 cd: as-disc AS 401 cd: history 205244/205142
los angeles 8-12 february 1961	columbia so	lp: columbia (usa) ML 5761/MS 6361 lp: cbs BRG 72097/SBRG 72097/ 60298 cd: sony MK 42038/MYK 44872/ SMK 64484

dvorak symphony no 9 "from the new world"
los angeles 16 july 1942	los angeles philharmonic	cd: dante LYS 415 cd: music and arts CD 788/CD 4788
los angeles 14-20 february 1959	columbia so	lp: columbia (usa) ML 5384/MS 6066/ Y-30045 lp: philips ABL 3291/SABL 152 lp: cbs BRG 72093/SBRG 72093 cd: sony MK 42039/MBK 44887/ SMK 64484

slavonic dance no 1
new york 4 february 1941	new york philharmonic	78: columbia (usa) X 211 78: columbia (canada) J 74 lp: columbia (usa) MT 48018 cd: sony SMK 64466/SX10K 66247

KARL GOLDMARK (1830-1915)

violin concerto no 1
new york	new york	lp: discocorp BWS 523
1 november	philharmonic	cd: as-disc AS 407
1942	milstein	cd: music and arts CD 972
		cd: one eleven (usa) URS 50140

GEORGE FRIDERIC HANDEL (1685-1759)

concerto grosso op 6 no 12
paris	paris	78: hmv DB 3601-3602
17 may	conservatoire	
1938	orchestra	

FRANZ JOSEF HAYDN (1732-1809)

symphony no 86

london 13 september 1938	london so	78: hmv DB 3647-3649 78: victor M 578 lp: discocorp BWS 999 cd: grammofono AB 78629
new york 18 march 1939	nbc so	cd: eklipse (japan) T 3
new york 12 december 1948	new york philharmonic	cd: as-disc AS 407 cd: historic performers HP 21

symphony no 88

new york 7 november 1943	new york philharmonic	cd: as-disc AS 407
los angeles 4-8 march 1961	columbia so	lp: columbia (usa) ML 5886/MS 6486 lp: cbs BRG 72141/SBRG 72141/ 60501 cd: sony MK 42047/MYK 44777/ SMK 64485

haydn **symphony no 92 "oxford"**

paris 7 may 1938	paris conservatoire orchestra	78: hmv DB 3559-3661 78: victor M 682 lp: victor CAL 257 lp: discocorp BWS 999 cd: dutton CDEA 5003 cd: grammofono AB 78629 cd: pearl GEMMCD 9945 cd: vai audio VAIA 1081 cd: history 205242/205241
new york 10 february 1940	nbc so	cd: eklipse (japan) T 3
boston 21 january 1947	boston so	cd: wing (japan) WCD 58 cd: historic performers HP 21

symphony no 96 "miracle"

vienna 3-5 may 1937	vienna philharmonic	78: hmv DB 3282-3284/ 　　　DB 8359-8361 auto 78: victor M 885 lp: victor LCT 6015 lp: emi 1C053 01456M lp: discocorp BWS 1002 lp: turnabout THS 65020 cd: pearl GEMMCD 9945 cd: preiser 90114 *also a private lp edition by preiser*
new york 29 november- 12 december 1954	new york philharmonic	lp: columbia (usa) ML 5059 lp: philips ABL 3123/GBL 5622 cd: sony SMK 64486
paris 12 may 1955	orchestre national	unpublished radio broadcast

haydn symphony no 100 "military"

vienna 10-15 january 1938	vienna philharmonic	78: hmv DB 3421-3423/ DB 8445-8447 auto 78: victor M 472 lp: victor CAL 257 lp: emi 1C053 01456M lp: turnabout THS 65029 lp: discocorp BWS 1002 cd: historic performers HP 21 cd: grammofono AB 78629 cd: preiser 90141 *also a private lp edition by preiser*

los angeles
2-4
march
1961
	columbia so	lp: columbia (usa) ML 5886/MS 6486
		lp: cbs BRG 72141/SBRG 72141/
		    60501
		cd: sony MK 42047/MYK 44777/
		    SMK 64485

symphony no 102

new york 18 february 1953	new york philharmonic	lp: columbia (usa) ML 4814/ML 5059 lp: philips ABL 3123/GBL 5622 cd: sony SMK 64485 cd: palladio PD 4198

die jahreszeiten, excerpt (welche labung für die sinne)

san francisco 18 april 1954	san francisco symphony mazzolini *sung in english*	lp: cls records CLS 2031

PAUL HINDEMITH (1895-1963)

sinfonia serena

new york	new york	cd: as-disc AS 421
15 february	philharmonic	cd: music and arts CD 714/CD 4714
1948		cd: history 205246/205241

GUSTAV MAHLER (1860-1911)

symphony no 1

new york 8 april 1939	nbc so	cd: eklipse (japan) T 6 cd: grammofono AB 78595
london 6 november 1947	london philharmonic	unpublished radio broadcast *music performance research centre*
new york 12 february 1950	new york philharmonic	lp: movimento musica 01.016 cd: as-disc AS 402 cd: legends LGD 106 cd: urania URN 22.141
new york 24-25 january 1954	new york philharmonic	lp: columbia (usa) ML 4958/SL 218 lp: philips ABL 3044/ABL 3222/ A01150L cd: sony MHK 63328
los angeles 14 january- 6 april 1961	columbia so	lp: columbia (usa) ML 5794/MS 6394/ Y-30047 lp: cbs BRG 72099/SBRG 72099/ 61116 cd: sony MK 42031/MYK 42600/ M2YK 45674/SM2K 64447/ SX10K 66246

mahler **symphony no 2 "resurrection"**

vienna 15 may 1948	vienna philharmonic wiener singverein cebotari anday	lp: discocorp BWS 367 cd: nuova era NE 2314-2315 cd: grammofono AB 78787-78788 cd: arlecchino ARL 177-178
new york 5 december 1948	new york philharmonic westminster choir conner watson	unpublished radio broadcast

new york
18 february
1957-
21 february
1958
	new york
	philharmonic
	westminster
	choir
	cundari
	forrester
		lp: columbia (usa) M2L-256/
		    M2S-601/Y2-30848
		lp: philips ABL 3245-3246/
		    SABL 189-190
		lp: cbs BRG 72052-72053/
		    SBRG 72052-72053/
		    61182-61183/77266
		cd: sony M2K 42032/M2YK 45674/
		    SM2K 64447

mahler **symphony no 4**

new york 10 may 1945	new york philharmonic halban	78: columbia LX 949-954 78: columbia (austria) LVX 21-26 78: columbia (usa) M 589 lp: columbia 33CX 1034 lp: columbia (france) 33FCX 198 lp: columbia (usa) ML 4031/3216 0026 lp: philips NBL 5038/GBL 5608/ L09406L lp: cbs 61357-61358/78222 cd: sony MPK 46450/SMK 64450
boston 25 march 1947	boston so halban	cd: dante LYS 315
salzburg 23 august 1950	vienna philharmonic seefried	cd: varese VCD 47228 cd: originals SH 836 cd: mca classics MCAD 42337 cd: arlecchino ARL 177-178 *final movement* cd: orfeo/salzburg festival SF 001
frankfurt 4 september 1950	museums- orchester kupper	cd: green hill (japan) GH 0001
den haag 4 june 1952	concertgebouw orchestra schwarzkopf	cd: globe 6905
new york 4 january 1953	new york philharmonic seefried	cd: music and arts CD 656/CD 4656

mahler symphony no 4/concluded

paris 12 may 1955	orchestre national stader	cd: nuova era NE 2233
vienna 6 november 1955	vienna philharmonic güden	cd: dg 435 3342/435 3212
vienna 29 may 1960	vienna philharmonic schwarzkopf	lp: discocorp BWS 705 lp: columbia (japan) OW 7214 cd: arkadia CD 767/CDGI 767 cd: wing (japan) WCD 1-2 cd: music and arts CD 705 *final movement* cd: verona 27075 *walter's final concert in europe and final concert with the vienna philharmonic*

mahler **symphony no 5**
new york	new york	78: columbia LCX 8019-8026
10 february	philharmonic	78: columbia (usa) M 718
1947		lp: columbia (usa) SL 171/3226 0016
		lp: philips ABL 3188-3189/L09407L-09408L
		lp: cbs 61357-61358
		cd: sony MPK 47683/SMK 64451
		cd: grammofono AB 78838-78839
		cd: history 205246/205241

adagietto
78: columbia (holland) LHX 5
45: philips ABE 10027/A409 058E

adagietto/symphony no 5
vienna	vienna	78: hmv DB 3406
10-15	philharmonic	78: victor 12319
january		lp: emi 1C147 01402-01403M
1938		lp: world records SH 193-194
		cd: dutton CDEA 5014
		cd: music and arts CD 749/CD 4749
		cd: pearl GEMMCD 9413
		cd: preiser 90114
		also a private lp edition by preiser

symphony no 9
vienna	vienna	78: hmv DB 3613-3622
15-16	philharmonic	78: victor M 726
january		lp: victor LCT 6015
1938		lp: emi 1C147 01402-01403M
		lp: world records SH 193-194
		cd: emi CDH 763 0292
		cd: dutton CDEA 5005
		cd: palladio PD 4172-4173

los angeles	columbia so	lp: columbia (usa) M2L-276/M2S-676/
16 january-		Y2-30308
6 february		lp: cbs BRG 72068-72069/
1961		SBRG 72068-72069/
		61369-61370/77275
		cd: sony M2K 42033/SMK 64452

rehearsal extracts
lp: columbia (usa) M2L-276/M2S-676/WM 1
lp: cbs BRG 72068-72069/
SBRG 72068-72069
cd: sony SMK 64452

mahler **kindertotenlieder**

london
4 october
1949
	vienna
	philharmonic
	ferrier
		78: columbia LX 8939-8941
		lp: columbia 33C 1009
		lp: columbia (france) 33FC 1033
		lp: columbia (germany) C 70086/
		   33WC 1009
		lp: columbia (usa) ML 2187/ML 4980/
		   3226 0016
		lp: emi HLM 7002/2C061 01209/
		   1C147 01402-01403M
		lp: cbs 60203/72317
		cd: emi CDH 761 0032/CDM 566 9112
		cd: gala GL 307

lieder eines fahrenden gesellen

london 15 may 1955	bbc so fischer-dieskau	unpublished radio broadcast

los angeles
30 june-
1 july
1960
	columbia so
	miller
		lp: columbia (usa) ML 5888/MS 6488/
		   M2L-255/M2S-617
		lp: cbs 61369-61370/72142
		cd: sony MK 42025/MYK 45503/
		   SM2K 64447

mahler **das lied von der erde**

vienna 24 may 1936	vienna philharmonic thorborg kullmann	78: columbia ROX 165-171/ LX 8025-8031 auto 78: columbia (usa) M 300 78: columbia (canada) D 124 lp: perennial 2004 lp: emi HLM 7007/1C047 01204M lp: angel 60191 cd: dutton CDEA 5014 cd: emi CDH 764 2972/CHS 764 2942 cd: palladio PD 4172-4173 cd: music and arts CD 749/CD 4749 cd: pearl GEMMCD 9413 cd: grammofono AB 78553
edinburgh 11 september 1947	vienna philharmonic ferrier pears	unpublished radio broadcast *tapes may be irretrievably lost*
new york 18 january 1948	new york philharmonic ferrier svanholm	cd: naxos 811.0029 cd: new york philharmonic mahler broadcasts

vienna
14-20
may
1952
	vienna
	philharmonic
	ferrier
	patzak
		lp: decca LXT 2721-2722/
		    LXT 5575-5576/LXT 6278/
		    ACL 305/AKF 1-7/414 1941
		lp: london (usa) LLP 625-626/
		    5069-5070/A 4212/R 23182/
		    STS 15200
		cd: decca 414 1942/433 3302/
		    433 3322/466 5762

mahler das lied von der erde/concluded

new york 22 february 1953	new york philharmonic nikolaidi svanholm	cd: as-disc AS 403 cd: music and arts CD 950
new york 16 april 1960	new york philharmonic forrester lewis	cd: curtain call (japan) CD 206

new york
18-25
april
1960
	new york
	philharmonic
	miller
	haefliger
		lp: columbia (usa) ML 5826/MS 6426/
		    M2L-255/M2S-617/Y-30043
		lp: cbs BRG 72126/SBRG 72126/
		    60503
		cd: sony MK 42034/MYK 45500/
		    SMK 64455

mahler **lieder und gesänge aus der jugendzeit: erinnerung; scheiden und meiden; nicht wiedersehen; ich ging mit lust; ablösung im sommer; hans und grete; frühlingsmorgen; starke einbildungskraft**

new york   halban   78: columbia (usa) M 909
16 december   walter, piano lp: columbia (usa) SL 171
1947   lp: philips ABL 3188
                                                    cd: dante LYS 315
                                                    cd: sony MPK 46450/SM2K 64450
                                                   cd: grammofono AB 78838-78839

ich atmet' einen linden duft/rückert-lieder

vienna   vienna   lp: decca LXT 2722/LW 5123/
14-20   philharmonic   ACL 318/AKF 1-7
may   ferrier   lp: london (usa) LLP 626/LD 9137/
1952   5069/A 4212/STS 15202
                                                   cd: decca 421 2992/433 4772/433 8022/
                                                   448 1502/455 2952

vienna   vienna   lp: discocorp BWS 705/RR 208/RR 537
29 may   philharmonic   lp: columbia (japan) OW 7214
1960   schwarzkopf   cd: arkadia CD 767/CDGI 767
                                                 cd: music and arts CD 705
                                                 cd: verona 27075
                                                 walter's final concert in europe and final
                                                 concert with the vienna philharmonic

64
mahler **ich bin der welt abhanden gekommen/rückert-lieder**

vienna 24 may 1936	vienna philharmonic thorborg	78: columbia LB 45/LC 23 78: columbia (usa) 4201M lp: emi HLM 7017/1C047 01204M lp: parnassus 4 lp: angel 60191 cd: emi CDH 764 2972/CMS 764 2942 cd: music and arts CD 4749 cd: pearl GEMMCD 9413 cd: dutton CDEA 5014

vienna
14-20
may
1952
	vienna
	philharmonic
	ferrier
		lp: decca LXT 2722/LW 5123/
		    ACL 318/AKF 1-7
		lp: london (usa) LLP 626/LD 9137/
		    5069/A 4212/STS 15202
		cd: decca 421 2992/433 4772/
		    433 8022/448 1502/455 2952

vienna 29 may 1960	vienna philharmonic schwarzkopf	lp: discocorp BWS 705/RR 208/RR 537 lp: columbia (japan) OW 7214 cd: arkadia CD 767/CDGI 767 cd: music and arts CD 705 cd: verona 27075 *walter's final concert in europe and final appearance with the vienna philharmonic*

mahler **um mitternacht/rückert-lieder**

vienna	vienna	lp: decca LXT 2722/LW 5123/
14-20	philharmonic	LW 5225/ACL 318/AKF 1-7/
may	ferrier	PA 172
1952		lp: london (usa) LLP 626/LD 9137/
		5069/A 4212/STS 15202
		cd: decca 421 2992/430 0962/
		433 4772/433 8022/448 1502/
		448 2952/458 8702

wo die schönen trompeten blasen/des knaben wunderhorn

vienna	vienna	lp: discocorp BWS 705/RR 208/
29 may	philharmonic	RR 537
1960	schwarzkopf	lp: columbia (japan) OW 7214
		cd: arkadia CD 767/CDGI 767
		cd: music and arts CD 705
		cd: verona 27075

walter's final concert in europe and final appearance with the vienna philharmonic

FELIX MENDELSSOHN-BARTHOLDY (1809-1847)

violin concerto

new york 7 march 1945	new york philharmonic milstein	us forces v-disc 696-698

new york 16 may 1945	new york philharmonic milstein	78: columbia (usa) M 577 78: columbia (canada) D 158 78: columbia (brazil) 30-5385/8 lp: columbia (usa) ML 4001 lp: discocorp BWS 716 cd: sony SMK 64459/SX10K 66246 cd: arkadia 78576 cd: dante LYS 338 cd: pearl GEMMCD 9259 cd: arlecchino ARLA 96-97 cd: magic talent MT 48018

new york 7 march 1947	new york philharmonic francescatti	lp: discocorp (japan) BWS 1025

a midsummer night's dream, overture

new york 12 december 1948	new york philharmonic	cd: music and arts CD 822/CD 4822 cd: wing (japan) WCD 36

mendelssohn a midsummer night's dream, nocturne

london 11 february 1925	orchestra of the royal philharmonic society	78: columbia L 1651 78: columbia (usa) 67086D cd: istituto discographico italiano IDIS 295-296
new york 12 december 1948	new york philharmonic	cd: music and arts CD 822/CD 4822 cd: wing (japan) WCD 36

a midsummer night's dream, scherzo

new york 16 may 1945	new york philharmonic	78: columbia (usa) M 577 lp: columbia (usa) ML 4001 cd: dante LYS 338
new york 12 december 1948	new york philharmonic	cd: music and arts CD 822/CD 4822 cd: wing (japan) WCD 36

the hebrides, overture

berlin august or october 1923	berlin philharmonic	78: grammophon 65930/69589 lp: dg 2740 259 cd: dg 459 0002/459 0652 cd: istituto discographico italiano IDIS 295-296
new york 15 february 1948	new york philharmonic	cd: music and arts CD 714/CD 4714

mendelssohn **die spinnerin/lieder ohne worte**

los angeles 2 july 1952	walter, piano	lp: discocorp BWS 807 cd: wing (japan) WCD 51

auf flügeln des gesanges

new york 12 february 1950	lehmann walter, piano	cd: eklipse EKR 47
san francisco 17 april 1950	lehmann walter, piano	lp: discocorp BWS 729/BWS 807 cd: eklipse EKR 20

die liebende schreibt

washington 2 april 1950	schumann walter, piano	lp: voce VOCE 117 lp: columbia (japan) OW 7225 cd: wing (japan) WCD 51

WOLFGANG AMADEUS MOZART (1756-1791)

symphony no 25

new york 10 december 1954	columbia so	lp: columbia (usa) ML 5002 lp: philips ABR 4060/GBL 5502/ 　　G03507L lp: cbs 61720 cd: sony SMK 64473
new york 11 march 1956	new york philharmonic	cd: nuova era NE 2259-2261
salzburg 26 july 1956	vienna philharmonic	lp: discocorp BWS 367 lp: sony (japan) SOCO 110 cd: orfeo C430 961B

symphony no 28

new york 3 december 1954	columbia so	lp: columbia (usa) ML 5002 lp: philips ABR 4060/GBL 5502/ 　　G03507L lp: cbs 61720 cd: sony SMK 64473
chicago 23 january 1957	chicago so	cd: chicago symphony CD 91/2

symphony no 29

new york 29-30 december 1954	columbia so	lp: columbia (usa) ML 5375 lp: philips GBL 5502/G03507L lp: cbs 61720 cd: sony SMK 64473
new york 4 march 1956	new york philharmonic	cd: wing (japan) WCD 46

mozart **symphony no 35 "haffner"**

new york 17 february 1939	nbc so	cd: eklipse (japan) T 1
boston 21 january 1947	boston so	cd: wing (japan) WCD 58
new york 4 january 1953	new york philharmonic	unpublished radio broadcast *music performance research centre*
new york 5 january 1953	new york philharmonic	lp: columbia (usa) ML 4693 lp: philips ABL 3155/A01173L cd: sony SMK 64473

los angeles
13-21
january
1959
	columbia so	lp: columbia (usa) M3L-291/
		    M3S-691/ML 5655/MS 6255
		lp: cbs BRG 72005/SBRG 72005/
		    77308
		lp: philips A01524L
		cd: sony MK 42026/MYK 44778/
		    M2YK 45676/SM3K 46511

one of these performances of the haffner symphony also appears on nuova era cd NE 2259-2261

mozart **symphony no 36 "linz"**

new york 26-28 april 1955	columbia so	*performance only* lp: columbia (usa) ML 5375 lp: philips A01271L *performance and rehearsal* lp: columbia (usa) DSL 224 lp: philips ABL 3161-3162/ A01254L-A01255L cd: sony SM2K 64473/SM3K 64121 *rehearsal only* cd: sony SM3K 46511
paris 14 june 1955	orchestre national	cd: cetra CDE 3010 cd: venezia V 1006 cd: virtuoso 269.7022 cd: nuova era NE 2259-2261

los angeles
28-29
february
1960
	columbia so	lp: columbia (usa) M3L-291/
		    M3S-691/ML 5893/MS 6493
		lp: cbs BRG 72137/SBRG 72137/
		    72304/77308
		cd: sony MK 42027/MYK 44826/
		    M2YK 45676/SM3K 46511

mozart **symphony no 38 "prague"**

vienna
5-18
december
1936
	vienna
	philharmonic
		78: hmv DB 3112-3114/
		    DB 8302-8304 auto
		78: victor M 457
		lp: hmv COLH 37
		lp: victor CAL 237/CFL 105
		lp: emi 1C147 50178-50180M/
		    MFP 2061
		lp: turnabout THS 65033-65035
		cd: emi CHS 763 9122
		cd: arkadia 78505
		cd: grammofono AB 78793
		cd: arlecchino ARL 195
		cd: pearl GEMMCD 9940
		cd: magic talent MT 48028
		cd: history 205242/205241

florence 25 may 1954	maggio musicale orchestra	cd: wing (japan) WCD 57
new york 6 december 1954	new york philharmonic	cd: sony SM2K 64474/SM3K 64121 *unpublished columbia lp recording*
paris 5 may 1955	orchestre national	lp: discocorp (japan) BWS 1026 cd: nuova era NE 2259-2261
vienna 6 november 1955	vienna philharmonic	cd: dg 435 3342/435 3212

los angeles
2 december
1959
	columbia so	lp: columbia (usa) M3L-291/
		    M3S-691/ML 5895/MS 6494
		lp: cbs BRG 72138/SBRG 72138/
		    77308
		cd: sony MK 42027/MYK 44826/
		    M2YK 45676/SM3K 46511

1958 radio broadcast with new york philharmonic may also survive

mozart **symphony no 39**

london 21-22 may 1934	bbc so	78: hmv DB 2258-2260 78: victor M 258 lp: victor CAL 237/CFL 105 cd: grammofono AB 78560 cd: arkadia 78505 cd: arlecchino ARL 195 cd: history 204553-308
new york 26 may 1946	new york philharmonic	v-disc 67
stockholm 8 september 1950	stockholm philharmonic	lp: olympic 8125 cd: bis BISCD 424
new york 21 december 1953	new york philharmonic	lp: columbia (usa) ML 5014 lp: philips ABL 3206 cd: sony SMK 64477/SM3K 64121 *recording completed on 5 march 1956*
new york 4 march 1956	new york philharmonic	cd: cetra CDE 3010 cd: virtuoso 269.7022
paris 14 june 1956	orchestre national	unpublished radio broadcast

los angeles
20-23
february
1960
	columbia so	lp: columbia (usa) M3L-291/
		    M3S-691/ML 5893/MS 6493
		lp: cbs BRG 72137/SBRG 72137/
		    77308
		cd: sony MK 42026/MYK 44778/
		    M2YK 45676/SM3K 46511

one of these performances of symphony no 39 also appears on nuova era cd NE 2259-2261

74
mozart **symphony no 40**

berlin january 1929	staatskapelle	78: columbia DX 31-33 78: columbia (australia) DOX 25-27 78: columbia (usa) M 182 lp: discocorp (japan) BWS 1003 cd: wing (japan) WCD 26
new york 11 march 1939	nbc so	cd: eklipse (japan) T 1
los angeles 12 june 1949	los angeles philharmonic	cd: eklipse (japan) T 2
new york 5 february 1950	new york philharmonic	lp: cls records CLS 2032 cd: palladio PD 4198
berlin 24 september 1950	berlin philharmonic	lp: discocorp BWS 726 cd: arkadia CD 738/CDGI 738 cd: music and arts CD 239 *final movement* lp: period SPL 716 lp: everest SDBR 3252 lp: columbia (japan) OS 7076 vhs video: teldec 4509 950386 laserdisc: teldec 4509 950386 *the lp issues of the final movement, taken from an unpublished film newsreel soundtrack, incorrectly described the conductor as furtwängler*

mozart symphony no 40/concluded

vienna 14-16 may 1952	vienna philharmonic	lp: sony (japan) SOCO 110/15AC 1497
den haag 4 june 1952	concertgebouw orchestra	lp: discocorp (japan) BWS 1022 cd: wing (japan) WCD 26 *discocorp edition is dated 1948*
new york 23 february 1953	new york philharmonic	lp: columbia (usa) ML 4693 lp: philips ABL 3155/A01173L cd: sony SMK 64477/SM3K 64121

los angeles
13-16
january
1959
	columbia so	lp: columbia (usa) M3L-291/
		    M3S-691/ML 5894/MS 6494
		lp: cbs BRG 72138/SBRG 72138/
		    77308
		cd: sony MK 42028/SBK 45978/
		    M2YK 45676/SM3K 46511

*one of these performances of symphony no 40 also appears on nuova era
cd NE 2259-2261*

mozart **symphony no 41 "jupiter"**

vienna
10-15
january
1938
	vienna
	philharmonic
		78: hmv DB 3428-3431/
		    DB 8135-8138 auto
		78: victor M 253
		lp: victor CAL 253/CFL 104/
		    CFL 105
		lp: hmv COLH 37
		lp: emi 1C147 50178-50180M/
		    MFP 2061
		cd: emi CHS 763 9122
		cd: palladio PD 4169
		cd: arlecchino ARL 195
		cd: preiser 90141
		cd: grammofono AB 78793
		cd: arkadia 78505
		cd: history 205242/205241
		also a private lp edition by preiser

new york 23 january 1945	new york philharmonic	lp: columbia 33CX 1082 lp: columbia (italy) 33QCX 10079 lp: columbia (usa) ML 4880 cd: dante LYS 338
new york 5 march 1956	new york philharmonic	lp: columbia (usa) ML 5014 lp: philips ABL 3206/A01271L cd: sony SMK 64477/SM3K 64121

los angeles
25-28
february
1960
	columbia so	lp: columbia (usa) M3L-291/
		    M3S-691/ML 5655/MS 6255
		lp: cbs BRG 72005/SBRG 72005/
		    77308
		lp: philips A01524L
		cd: sony MK 42028/M2YK 45676/
		    SM3K 46511

mozart **piano concerto no 14**
new york	new york	lp: discocorp BWS 36
17 january	philharmonic	lp: penzance PR 36
1954	hess	cd: as-disc AS 401
		cd: historic performers HP 9
		cd: music and arts CD 275

piano concerto no 20
vienna	vienna	78: hmv DB 3273-3276/
7 may	philharmonic	DB 8544-8547 auto
1937	walter, pianist	78: victor M 420
	and conductor	lp: victor LM 6130
		lp: hmv COLH 36
		lp: rococo 2065
		lp: turnabout THS 65036
		lp: emi 1C147 50178-50180M
		cd: preiser 90141
		cd: wing (japan) WCD 50
		cd: emi CHS 763 9122
		cd: pearl GEMMCD 9940
		cd: magic talent MT 48028
new york	nbc so	cd: eklipse (japan) T 1
11 march	walter, pianist	cd: as-disc AS 404
1939	and conductor	cd: grammofono AB 78622
		cd: history 205242/205241
new york	new york	lp: cls records CLS 2032
5 february	philharmonic	
1950	firkusny	
new york	new york	lp: discocorp BWS 36
4 march	philharmonic	lp: penzance PR 36
1956	hess	cd: as-disc AS 401
		cd: historic performers HP 9
		cd: nuova era NE 2259-2261
		cd: music and arts CD 275

mozart **piano concerto no 22**

new york	new york	lp: piano archives MJA 1969
13-16	philharmonic	lp: discocorp BWS 717
november	schnabel	cd: as-disc AS 405
1941		cd: music and arts CD 681
		cd: radio years RY 69

piano concerto no 23

los angeles	los angeles	cd: as-disc AS 412
12 june	philharmonic	cd: eklipse (japan) T 2
1949	fleisher	

violin concerto no 3

new york	nbc so	cd: as-disc AS 416
24 february	szigeti	cd: music and arts CD 720
1950		*AS 416 includes rehearsal extracts*

los angeles	columbia so	lp: columbia (usa) ML 5381/MS 6063
10-17	francescatti	lp philips SABL 150/A01426L
december		lp: cbs 72323
1958		cd: sony MK 42030/MPK 52526/ SMK 64468

mozart **violin concerto no 4**

new york 16 december 1945	new york philharmonic huberman	lp: raritas OPR 402 lp: discocorp RR 551 lp: rococo 2026 cd: music and arts CD 299/CD 4299
new york 26 may 1946	new york philharmonic huberman	unpublished radio broadcast
los angeles 10-17 december 1958	columbia so francescatti	lp: columbia (usa) ML 5381/MS 6063 lp: philips SABL 150/A01426L/ 610 306R lp: cbs 72323 cd: sony MK 42030/SMK 64468

violin concerto no 5

new york 26 december 1954	new york philharmonic szigeti	cd: wing (japan) WCD 27

sinfonia concertante for violin and viola

new york 10 march 1946	new york philharmonic corigliano lincer	lp: discocorp BWS 523 cd: as-disc AS 405 cd: radio years RY 69

divertimento no 15

new york 11 march 1939	nbc so	cd: as-disc AS 404 cd: eklipse (japan) T 1 cd: grammofono AB 78622

mozart **maurerische trauermusik**

new york 2-30 december 1954	columbia so	lp: columbia (usa) ML 5004 lp: philips ABL 3118/A01237L/ GBL 5552 cd: sony SMK 64486
paris 14 june 1956	orchestre national	cd: venezia (japan) V 1006 cd: memories HR 4587

los angeles
8-31
march
1961
	columbia so	lp: columbia (usa) ML 5756/MS 6356/
		   Y-30048
		lp: cbs BRG 72043/SBRG 72043
		cd: sony MK 42029/MYK 42593/
		   SBK 45978

serenade no 7 "haffner"

boston 1944	boston so	unpublished radio broadcast

mozart **serenade no 13 "eine kleine nachtmusik"**

london april 1932	british so	78: columbia LX 144-145 78: columbia (italy) GQX 10699-10700 78: columbia (usa) X 19
vienna 5-18 december 1936	vienna philharmonic	78: hmv DB 3075-3076 78: victor M 364 lp: victor CAL 253/CFL 105 lp: hmv COLH 36 lp: emi 1C147 50178-50180M lp: turnabout THS 65036 cd: emi CHS 763 9122 cd: pearl GEMMCD 9940 cd: grammofono AB 78528 cd: magic talent MT 48028
stockholm 8 september 1950	stockholm philharmonic	lp: olympic OL 8125 lp: discocorp BWS 207
san francisco 18 april 1954	san francisco symphony	lp: cls records CLS 2031 cd: eklipse (japan) T 2
new york 2-30 december 1954	columbia so	45: philips ABE 10023/A409 021E 45: philips (france) 99 843DE lp: columbia (usa) ML 5004 lp: philips ABL 3118/A01237L/ GBL 5552/GBR 6513/G05617R cd: sony SM2K 64468
paris 14 june 1956	orchestre national	cd: venezia (japan) V 1006 cd: virtuoso 269.7022
los angeles 17 december 1958	columbia so	lp: columbia (usa) ML 5756/MS 6356/ Y-30048 lp: cbs BRG 72043/SBRG 72043 cd: sony MK 42029/MYK 42593

82
mozart **3 german dances k605**

vienna 3-5 may 1937	vienna philharmonic	78: hmv DA 1570 78: victor 4564 lp: emi 1C147 50178-50180M lp: turnabout THS 65036 cd: emi CHS 763 9122 cd: pearl GEMMCD 9940 cd: magic talent MT 48028
los angeles 21 may 1950	los angeles philharmonic	cd: eklipse EKR 1402 cd: eklipse (japan) T 2
new york 2-30 december 1954	columbia so	45: philips ABE 10027/A409 058E lp: columbia (usa) ML 5004 lp: philips ABL 3118/A01237L/ 　　GBL 5552/G03544L cd: sony SMK 64486

2 minuets from cassation in g

new york 9 march 1940	nbc so	cd: eklipse (japan) T 2

2 minuets from k568 and k599

new york 2-30 december 1954	columbia so	lp: columbia (usa) ML 5004 lp: philips ABL 3118/A01237L/ 　　GBL 5552/G03544L cd: sony SMK 64486

mozart **requiem**

paris 29 june 1937	vienna philharmonic vienna opera chorus schumann thorborg dermota kipnis	lp: ed smith UORC 251 lp: emi EG 29 07811 cd: emi CHS 763 9122 cd: grammofono AB 78546 cd: arkadia 78528 *excerpts* cd: history 30.3075
new york 9 november 1941	new york philharmonic westminster choir steber szantho hain moscona	cd: wing (japan) WCD 54

new york
10-12
march
1956
	new york
	philharmonic
	westminster
	choir
	seefried
	tourel
	simoneau
	warfield
		lp: columbia (usa) ML 5012/Y-34619/
		    M3P 39651
		lp: philips A01251L
		lp: cbs 72326
		cd: sony MPK 45556/SM3K 47211/
		    SMK 64480
		cd: historical performers HP 12

vienna 23 june 1956	vienna philharmonic wiener singverein lipp rössl-majdan dermota edelmann	lp: sony (japan) SOC0 111/20AC 1961

mozart requiem/concluded

salzburg 26 july 1956	vienna philharmonic vienna opera chorus della casa malaniuk dermota siepi	lp: cetra LO 516 cd: nuova era NE 2209 cd: orfeo C430 961B

lacrymosa/requiem

chicago 13 march 1958	chicago so and chorus	cd: chicago symphony orchestra CD 98-2

et incarnatus est/mass in c minor

san francisco 18 april 1954	san francisco symphony mazzolini	lp: cls records CLS 2031

exsultate jubilate

new york december 1953	new york philharmonic seefried	cd: stradivarius STR 10006

mozart **alleluia/exsultate jubilate**

new york	orchestra	78: columbia (usa) 17347D
11 may	pons	78: columbia (australia) LO 76
1942		lp: columbia (usa) ML 4217
		cd: sony SM3K 47211

mentre ti lascio o figlia, concert aria

new york	metropolitan	78: columbia (usa) M 643
7 february	opera orchestra	45: philips ABE 10018/A409 027E
1947	pinza	lp: columbia (usa) ML 4036/
		ML 5239/Y-54085/3216 0335
		cd: sony MPK 45693/SM3K 47211
		cd: cantus classics CACD 500042

new york	columbia so	lp: columbia (usa) ML 4699
7-8	london	cd: sony SM3K 47211
may		
1953		

per questa bella mano, concert aria

new york	columbia so	lp: columbia (usa) ML 4699
7-8	london	cd: sony SM3K 47211
may		
1953		

rivolgete a lui lo sguardo, concert aria

new york	columbia so	lp: columbia (usa) ML 4699
7-8	london	cd: sony SM3K 47211
may		
1953		

mozart **das veilchen**

washington	schumann	lp: voce records VOCE 117
2 april	walter, piano	lp: columbia (japan) OW 7225
1950		cd: wing (japan) WCD 51

la clemenza di tito, overture

vienna	vienna	78: hmv DB 6032
10-15	philharmonic	78: victor 12506
january		lp: rococo 2065
1938		lp: emi 1C147 50178-50180M
		cd: emi CHS 763 9122

cosi fan tutte, overture

berlin	staatskapelle	78: grammophon 66072
march		lp: discocorp (japan) BWS 1004
1925		
new york	new york	78: columbia (usa) M 565
january	philharmonic	lp: columbia (usa) A 1065
1945		lp: penzance PR 36
		penzance issue dated 1954
new york	columbia so	45: philips A409023E
2-30		lp: columbia (usa) ML 5004
december		lp: philips ABL 3118/A01237L/
1954		GBL 5552/G03544L
		cd: sony SMK 64486
los angeles	columbia so	lp: columbia (usa) ML 5756/MS 6356/
29-31		Y-30048
march		lp: cbs BRG 72043/SBRG 72043
1961		cd: sony MK 42029/MYK 42593

mozart cosi fan tutte, excerpt (per pieta)

new york	columbia so	lp: columbia (usa) ML 4694/3216 0363
14-21	steber	cd: sony SM3K 47211
february		
1953		

don giovanni

salzburg	vienna	lp: raritas OPR 1408
2 august	philharmonic	lp: discocorp BWS 802
1937	vienna opera	cd: radio years RY 83-85
	chorus	cd: eklipse EKR 43
	rethberg	*excerpts*
	helletsgruber	lp: ed smith UORC 105
	bokor	lp: amadeo 427 0891
	borgioli	cd: amadeo 427 0892
	pinza	cd: orfeo C394 101B/C408 955R
	lazzari	
	ettl	
	alsen	
new york	metropolitan	lp: discocorp WSA 305/BWS 304
7 march	opera orchestra	lp: cls records CLS 32017
1942	and chorus	cd: nuova era NE 2275-2277
	novotma	cd: great opera performances GOP 798
	bampton	cd: naxos 811.0013-811.0014
	sayao	cd: memories HR 4225-4227
	kullmann	
	pinza	
	kipnis	

don giovanni, excerpt (fragment from act one)

salzburg	vienna	cd: eklipse EKR 43
1 august	philharmonic	
1935	arangi-lombardi	

mozart **don giovanni, excerpt (madamina!)**

new york	metropolitan	78: columbia (usa) M 643
7 february	opera orchestra	78: columbia (australia) LOX 615
1947	pinza	45: philips ABE 10015/A409 026E
		lp: columbia (usa) ML 4036/ML 5239/ Y-54085/3216 0335
		lp: philips GBL 5577
		cd: sony MPK 45693/SM3K 47211
		cd: cantus classics CACD 500042

don giovanni, excerpt (mi tradi)

new york	columbia so	lp: columbia (usa) ML 4694/3216 0363
14-21	steber	cd: sony SM3K 47211
february		
1953		

don giovanni, excerpt (non mi dir)

new york	columbia so	lp: columbia (usa) ML 4694/3216 0363
14-21	steber	cd: sony SM3K 47211
february		
1953		

die entführung aus dem serail, excerpt (traurigkeit ward mir zum lose)

new york	columbia so	lp: columbia (usa) ML 4694/3216 0363
14-21	steber	cd: sony SM3K 47211
february		
1953		

mozart die entführung aus dem serail, excerpt (ach ich liebte)

new york	orchestra	78: columbia LB 20002
11 may	pons	78: columbia (australia) LO 79
1942	*sung in french*	78: columbia (usa) 17346D
		lp: columbia (usa) ML 4217/Y-31152
		cd: sony SM3K 47211

die entführung aus dem serail, excerpt (welche wonne, welche lust!)

new york	orchestra	78: columbia LB 20003
11 may	pons	78: columbia (australia) LO 76
1942	*sung in french*	78: columbia (usa) 17347D
		lp: columbia (usa) ML 4217/Y-31152
		cd: sony SM3K 47211

die entführung aus dem serail, excerpt (ha wie will ich triumphieren!)

new york	metropolitan	78: victor M 643
7 february	opera orchestra	45: philips ABE 10018/A409 027E
1947	pinza	lp: columbia (usa) ML 4036/Y-54085/
	sung in italian	3216 0335
		lp: philips GBL 5577
		cd: sony MPK 45693/SM3K 47211
		cd: cantus classics CACD 500042

la finta giardiniera, overture

vienna	vienna	78: hmv DB 3431/DB 6032/DB 8132
10-15	philharmonic	78: victor 12526
january		lp: rococo 2065
1938		lp: emi 1C147 50178-50180M
		cd: emi CHS 763 9122

idomeneo, overture

berlin	staatskapelle	78: grammophon 66072
march		lp: discocorp BWS 1004
1925		cd: wing (japan) WCD 29

mozart **le nozze di figaro**

salzburg	vienna	lp: discocorp RR 801
11 august	philharmonic	cd: arkadia 50004
1937	vienna opera	*excerpts*
	chorus	orfeo C394 101B/C408 955R
	rautawaara	
	rethy	
	novotna	
	pinza	
	stabile	
new york	metropolitan	lp: discocorp MLG 75-77
29 january	opera orchestra	lp: operatic archives OPA 1033-1035
1944	and chorus	cd: as-disc AS 419-420
	steber	*excerpts*
	sayao	cd: legato BIM 712
	novotna	
	pinza	
	brownlee	

le nozze di figaro, excerpt (voi che sapete)

new york	orchestra	78: columbia LB 20001
11 may	pons	78: columbia (usa) M 518
1942	*sung in french*	lp: columbia (usa) ML 4217
		cd: sony SM3K 47211

mozart **le nozze di figaro, excerpt (se vuol ballare)**

new york	metropolitan	78: columbia (usa) M 643
7 february	opera orchestra	45: philips ABE 10015/A409 026E
1947	pinza	lp: columbia (usa) ML 4036/ML 5239
		Y-54085/3216 0335
		cd: sony MPK 45693/SM3K 47211
		cd: cantus classics CACD 500042

new york	columbia so	lp: columbia (usa) ML 4699
7-8 may	london	cd: sony SM3K 47211
1953		

le nozze di figaro, excerpt (la vendetta!)

new york	columbia so	lp: columbia (usa) ML 4699
7-8 may	london	cd: sony SM3K 47211
1953		

le nozze di figaro, excerpt (non piu andrai)

new york	columbia so	lp: columbia (usa) ML 4699
7-8 may	london	cd: sony SM3K 47211
1953		

le nozze di figaro, excerpt (hai gia vinta la causa!)

new york	columbia so	lp: columbia (usa) ML 4699
7-8 may	london	cd: sony SM3K 47211
1953		

le nozze di figaro, excerpt (dove sono)

new york	columbia so	lp: columbia (usa) ML 4694/
14-21	steber	3216 0363/30053
february		cd: sony MDK 46579/SM3K 47211
1953		cd: metropolitan opera MET 211

le nozze di figaro, excerpt (aprite un po quegli' occhi)

new york	metropolitan	78: columbia (usa) M 643
7 february	opera orchestra	lp: columbia (usa) ML 4036/ML 5239/
1947	pinza	Y-54085/3216 0335
		cd: sony MPK 45693/SM3K 47211
		cd: cantus classics CACD 500042

new york	columbia so	lp: columbia (usa) ML 4699
7-8 may	london	cd: sony SM3K 47211
1953		

mozart **le nozze di figaro, overture**

london 15 april 1932	british so	78: columbia LX 232/LCX 18 78: columbia (france) LFX 329 78: columbia (australia) LOX 180 cd: toshiba TOCE 7322
los angeles 12 june 1949	los angeles philharmonic	cd: eklipse (japan) T 2
stockholm 8 september 1950	stockholm philharmonic	lp: olympic OL 8125
new york 24 february 1951	nbc so	lp: columbia (japan) OZ 7509 cd: as-disc AS 416
new york 2-30 december 1954	columbia so	lp: columbia (usa) ML 5004 lp: philips ABL 3118/A01237L/ GBL 5552/G03544L cd: sony SMK 64486
los angeles 29-31 march 1961	columbia so	lp: columbia (usa) ML 5756/MS 6356/ Y-30048 lp: cbs BRG 72043/SBRG 72043 cd: sony MK 42029/MYK 42593

mozart **il re pastore, excerpt (l'amero saro costante)**

new york	orchestra	78: columbia 71696D
11 may	pons	lp: columbia ML 4217
1942		cd: sony SM3K 47211

der schauspieldirektor, overture

new york	columbia so	45: philips ABE 10010/A409023E
2-30		lp: columbia (usa) ML 5004
december		lp: philips ABL 3118/A01237L/
1954		GBL 5552/G03544L
		cd: sony SMK 64486

los angeles	columbia so	lp: columbia (usa) ML 5756/MS 6356/
29-31		Y-30048
march		lp: cbs BRG 72043/SBRG 72043
1961		cd: sony MK 42029/MYK 42593

der schauspieldirektor, excerpt (bester jüngling!)

new york	columbia so	lp: columbia (usa) ML 4694/3216 0363
14-21	steber	cd: sony SM3K 47211
february		
1953		

mozart **die zauberflöte**

new york 10 january 1942	metropolitan opera orchestra and chorus novotna bok bodanya kullmann kipnis brownlee schorr *sung in english*	unpublished met broadcast
new york 26 december 1942	metropolitan opera orchestra and chorus novotna antoine raymondi kullmann pinza brownlee cordon *sung in english*	lp: private issue MJA 5000 cd: walhall WHL 2
new york 1 april 1944	metropolitan opera orchestra and chorus conner bowman raymondi kullmann kipnis brownlee moscona *sung in english*	unpublished met broadcast

mozart die zauberflöte/concluded

new york 1 december 1945	metropolitan opera orchestra and chorus conner benzell raymondi kullmann pinza thompson ezekiel *sung in english*	unpublished met broadcast
new york 3 march 1956	metropolitan opera orchestra and chorus amara peters sullivan uppmann london hines *sung in english*	lp: cls records ARPCL 32018 lp: discocorp (japan) BWS 1018 cd: as-disc AS 425-426

performance issued on lp by historical recording enterprises HRE 316 and described as a 1949 metropolitan opera broadcast conducted by walter is in fact a 1950 performance conducted by fritz stiedry

die zauberflöte, fragmentary excerpts

salzburg 8 august 1931	vienna philharmonic gerhart mayr	lp: danacord DACO 131-133

mozart **die zauberflöte, excerpt (ach ich fühl's)**

new york	columbia so	lp: columbia (usa) ML 4694/3216 0363
14-21	steber	cd: sony SM3K 47211
february		
1953		

die zauberflöte, excerpt (in diesen heiligen hallen)

new york	metropolitan	78: columbia (usa) M 643
7 february	opera orchestra	45: philips ABE 10018/A409 027E
1947	pinza	lp: columbia (usa) ML 4036/Y-54085/
	sung in italian	3216 0335
		lp: philips GBL 5577
		cd: sony MPK 45693/SM3K 47211
		cd: cantus classics CACD 500042

die zauberflöte, excerpt (der hölle rache)

new york	orchestra	78: columbia LB 20001
11 may	pons	78: columbia (usa) M 518
1942	*sung in french*	lp: columbia (usa) ML 4217
		cd: sony SM3K 47211

metropolitan opera on record by frederick fellers (greenwood press 1984) gives recording dates of mozart arias recorded by walter and pinza as 21 february 1946 (mentre ti lascio and don giovanni) and 17 april 1946 (zauberflöte, entführung and nozze di figaro) mozart **die zauberflöte, overture**

paris june 1928	mozart festival orchestra	78: columbia 12549 78: columbia (usa) 67660D lp: discocorp (japan) BWS 1006
new york 2-30 december 1954	columbia so	45: philips A409023E lp: columbia (usa) ML 5004 lp: philips ABL 3118/A01237L/ GBL 5552/G03544L cd: sony SMK 64486
los angeles 29-31 march 1961	columbia so	lp: columbia (usa) ML 5756/MS 6356/ Y-30048 lp: cbs BRG 72043/SBRG 72043 cd: sony MK 42029/MYK 42593

GIOVANNI PALESTRINA (1525-1594)

stabat mater
paris   vienna opera   unpublished acetate recording
29 june   chorus
1937

HANS PFITZNER (1869-1949)

palestrina, excerpts
vienna   vienna   cd: koch 3-1457-2
14 october   philharmonic
1937   vienna opera
                  chorus
                  bokor
                  rethy
                  witt
                  wernigk
                  jerger
                  alsen

MAURICE RAVEL (1875-1937)

piano concerto for the left hand
amsterdam   concertgebouw   cd: as-disc AS 418
28 february   orchestra   cd: grammofono AB 78532
1937   wittgenstein   cd: urania URN 22.126

rapsodie espagnole
new york   nbc so   unpublished radio broadcast
24 february
1940

FRANZ SCHUBERT (1797-1828)

symphony no 5

new york 10 february 1940	nbc so	cd: eklipse (japan) T 4
new york 5-8 october 1955	columbia so	lp: columbia (usa) ML 5156 lp: philips ABL 3288/A01433L

los angeles
26 february-
3 march
1960
	columbia so	lp: columbia (usa) ML 5618/MS 6218/
		    M2L-268/M2S-618
		lp: philips SABL 209/835 575AY
		lp: cbs BRG 72084/SBRG 72084/
		    77263
		cd: sony MK 42048/SBK 60267/
		    SMK 64487/SX9K 66249

schubert **symphony no 8 "unfinished"**

vienna 18-21 may 1936	vienna philharmonic	78: hmv DB 2937-2939/ 　　DB 8187-8189 auto 78: victor G 9 cd: emi CDH 764 2962/CHS 764 2942 cd: palladio PD 4169 cd: arlecchino ARLA 52 cd: pearl GEMMCD 9945 *issued on lp in japan by toshiba*
philadelphia 2 march 1947	philadelphia orchestra	78: columbia (usa) M 699 lp: columbia 33CX 1082 lp: columbia (italy) 33QCX 10079 lp: columbia (usa) ML 2010/ML 4880 cd: grammofono AB 78805-78806 cd: history 205243/205241
new york 3 march 1958	new york philharmonic	lp: columbia (usa) ML 5618/ML 5906/ 　　MS 6218/MS 6506/M2L-269/ 　　M2S-618/Y-30314 lp: philips SABL 209/835 575AY lp: cbs BRG 72084/SBRG 72084/ 　　77263 cd: sony MK 42048/SMK 64487/ 　　SX9K 66249
chicago 13 march 1958	chicago so	cd: chicago symphony orchestra 　　CD 0001-0002
new york 16 april 1960	new york philharmonic	cd: wing (japan) WCD 27
vienna 29 may 1960	vienna philharmonic	lp: discocorp BWS 705 lp: columbia (japan) OW 7214 cd: arkadia CD 767/CDGI 767 cd: music and arts CD 705 *walter's final concert in europe and final* *concert with the vienna philharmonic*

schubert **symphony no 9 "great"**

paris 5-6 may 1938	conservatoire orchestra	hmv unpublished
london 11-12 september 1938	london so	78: hmv DB 3607-3612/ DB 8557-8562 auto 78: victor M 602 78: columbia (japan) JS 107-112 lp: victor CAL 195 lp: discocorp BWS 727 lp: turnabout THS 65170 cd: dutton CDEA 5003 cd: grammofono AB 78548 cd: arlecchino ARLA 52 *CAL 195 did not name conductor or orchestra*
new york 24 february 1940	nbc so	cd: eklipse (japan) T 3
new york 22 april 1946	new york philharmonic	78: columbia (usa) M 679 lp: columbia (usa) ML 4093 lp: philips ABL 3074/A00152L/ GBL 5609 cd: dante LYS 509
stockholm 8 september 1950	stockholm philharmonic	lp: olympic OL 8123 lp: discocorp BWS 207 lp: quadrifoglio VDS 9456 lp: eurodisc XAK 27164 cd: as-disc AS 306/AS 432 cd: historical performers HP 40

los angeles
31 january-
6 february
1959
	columbia so	lp: columbia (usa) ML 5619/MS 6219/
		    M2L-269/M2S-618/Y-34620
		lp: cbs BRG 72020/SBRG 72020/
		    61058/77263
		cd: sony MK 42049/MYK 44828/
		    SMK 64478/SX10K 66248

schubert **rosamunde overture**

new york 7 may 1944	new york philharmonic	cd: as-disc AS 417
edinburgh 13 september 1947	vienna philharmonic	cd: wing (japan) WCD 50 *recording incomplete*
new york 6-8 october 1955	columbia so	lp: columbia (usa) ML 5156 lp: philips GBL 5629/GBR 6513/ G05617R cd: sony SMK 64478/SX10K 66248

rosamunde, entr'acte in b minor (ballet music no 1)

london 12 september 1938	london so	78: hmv DB 3651 78: victor 12534 cd: dutton CDEA 5003

rosamunde, entr'acte in b flat

new york 6-8 october 1955	columbia so	lp: columbia (usa) ML 5156/DP 1 lp: philips GBL 5629/GBR 6513/ G05617R cd: sony SMK 64478/SX10K 66248

schubert **rosamunde, ballet in g (ballet music no 2)**

london 12 september 1938	london so	78: hmv DB 3651 78: victor 12534 cd: dutton CDEA 5003
new york 7 may 1944	new york philharmonic	cd: as-disc AS 417
new york 6-8 october 1955	columbia so	lp: columbia (usa) ML 5156/DP 1 lp: philips GBL 5629/GBR 6513/ G03520L/G05617R cd: sony SMK 64478/SX10K 66248

lieder: die junge nonne; romanze aus rosamunde; du liebst mich nicht; der tod und das mädchen; suleika I; du bist die ruh'

edinburgh 7 september 1949	ferrier walter, piano	lp: discocorp BWS 707 lp: decca 6BB 197-198/414 6111 cd: decca 414 6112/433 4762/433 8022 *romanze aus rosamunde also on decca* *cd 458 8702*

lieder: geheimes; wanderers nachtlied; hin und wider fliegen pfeile; mignon IV; liebe schwärmt auf allen wegen; schweizerlied; liebhaber in allen gestalten

washington 2 april 1950	schumann walter, piano	lp: voce VOCE 117 lp: columbia (japan) OW 7225 cd: wing (japan) WCD 51

schubert **mignon III (so lasst mich scheinen)**

washington 2 april 1950	schumann walter, piano	cd: wing (japan) WCD 50

ständchen (leise flehen meine lieder)

new york 12 february 1950	lehmann walter, piano	cd: eklipse EKR 47
san francisco 17 april 1950	lehmann walter, piano	lp: discocorp BWS 729/BWS 807 cd: eklipse EKR 20

liebesbotschaft/schwanengesang

new york 1950	lehmann walter, piano	lp: discocorp BWS 807

moment musical no 6

los angeles 2 july 1952	walter, piano	lp: discocorp BWS 807 cd: wing (japan) WCD 50

ROBERT SCHUMANN (1810-1856)

symphony no 1 "spring"
new york	new york	lp: discocorp BWS 716
16 december	philharmonic	cd: as-disc AS 413
1945		cd: iron needle IN 1353-1354

symphony no 3 "rhenish"
new york	new york	78: columbia (switzerland) LZX 230-233
4 february	philharmonic	78: columbia (usa) M 464
1941		lp: columbia 33CX 1045
		lp: columbia (france) 33FCX 147
		lp: columbia (usa) ML 4040
		lp: parnassus 7205
		lp: discocorp BWS 709
		cd: sony SMK 64488
		cd: grammofono AB 78532
		cd: iron needle IN 1357
		cd: arlecchino ARLA 53
		cd: historic performers HP 17
		cd: history 205244/205241

symphony no 4
paris	mozart	78: columbia L 2209-2212
19 june	festival	78: columbia (usa) M 106
1928	orchestra	cd: grammofono AB 78580
		cd: vai audio VAIA 1059

london	london so	78: hmv DB 3793-3795
26 april		78: victor M 837
1939		cd: iron needle IN 1357
		cd: arlecchino ARLA 53

new york	nbc so	lp: parnassus 7205
2 march		lp: discocorp BWS 709
1940		cd: as-disc AS 413
		cd: iron needle IN 1353-1354
		cd: music and arts CD 248/CD 4273
		cd: grammofono AB 78525

schumann **piano concerto**

los angeles 20-25 january 1960	columbia so istomin	lp: columbia (usa) ML 5494/MS 6159 lp: philips 610 302VR cd: sony MK 42024/MYK 44771/ SMK 64489

manfred overture

berlin march 1925	staatskapelle	78: grammophon 66074
chicago 1 february 1956	chicago so	cd: chicago symphony orchestra CD 0001-0002

frauenliebe und –leben, song cycle

new york 24 june 1941	lehmann walter, piano	78: columbia (usa) M 539 lp: columbia (usa) ML 2182/ML 4788/ 3216 0315 lp: philips A01265L lp: cbs 61501 cd: sony MPK 44840 cd: vocal archives VA 1158
edinburgh 7 september 1949	ferrier walter, piano	lp: discocorp DIS 3700/BWS 707 lp: decca 6BB 197-198/414 6111 cd: decca 414 6112/433 4762/433 8022

schumann **dichterliebe, song cycle**

new york	lehmann	78: columbia (usa) M 486
13 august	walter, piano	lp: columbia 33C 1020
1941		lp: columbia (france) 33FC 1034
		lp: columbia (usa) ML 2183/ML 4788/ 3216 0315
		lp: philips A01265L
		lp: cbs 61501
		cd: sony MPK 44840
		cd: vocal archives VA 1158

aufträge (nicht so schnelle, nicht so schnelle!)

new york	lehmann	cd: eklipse EKR 47
12 february	walter, piano	
1950		
san francisco	lehmann	lp: discocorp BWS 1009
17 april	walter, piano	
1950		

singet nicht in trauertönen

washington	schumann	lp: voce VOCE 117
2 april	walter, piano	lp: columbia (japan) OW 7225
1950		cd: wing (japan) WCD 51

2 pieces from kreisleriana: sehr langsam; sehr innig und nicht zu rasch

los angeles	walter, piano	lp: discocorp BWS 807
2 july		cd: wing (japan) WCD 51
1952		

BEDRICH SMETANA (1824-1884)

the moldau/ma vlast

new york 4 february 1941	new york philharmonic	78: columbia (usa) X 211 78: columbia (canada) J 74 lp: columbia (usa) ML 2075 lp: philips G03520L cd: sony SMK 64467/SX10K 66247 cd: grammofono AB 78805-78806 cd: magic talent CD 48018 cd: history 205244/205241
los angeles 19 june 1949	los angeles philharmonic	cd: music and arts CD 788/CD 4788

the bartered bride, overture

london 12 september 1938	london so	78: hmv DB 3562 cd: grammofono AB 78548 cd: magic talent CD 48018
new york 2 march 1940	nbc so	cd: grammofono AB 78622 cd: as-disc AS 404 cd: historic collector (japan) MM 37040 cd: history 205244/205241 *historic collector incorrectly dated 4 february 1941*
los angeles 19 june 1949	los angeles philharmonic	cd: music and arts CD 788/CD 4788

JOHN STAFFORD SMITH

the star-spangled banner, march

new york 11 july 1943	new york philharmonic	unpublished radio broadcast
philadelphia 12 february 1944	philadelphia orchestra	cd: wing (japan) WCD 49
new york 17 march 1945	metropolitan opera orchestra	cd: wing (japan) WCD 105-106

JOHANN STRAUSS (1825-1899)

an der schönen blauen donau, waltz
new york	columbia so	lp: columbia (usa) ML 5113/DP 1
22-23		lp: philips GBL 5551/GBR 6510/
march		G03520L/G03543L/G05613R
1956		lp: cbs 60505/61510
		cd: sony SMK 64467/SX10K 66247

die fledermaus, overture
berlin	staatskapelle	78: columbia L 2311
10-11		78: columbia (usa) 9080M
january		78: columbia (canada) 15131
1929		78: columbia (argentina) 264805
		lp: discocorp (japan) BWS 1003
		cd: dante LYS 358
paris	conservatoire	78: hmv DB 3536
9 may	orchestra	78: victor M 805
1938		lp: discocorp (japan) BWS 1006
		cd: dante LYS 358
		cd: pearl GEMMCD 9945
new york	new york	cd: as-disc AS 417
5 july	philharmonic	
1944		
edinburgh	vienna	cd: wing (japan) WCD 3-4
13 september	philharmonic	
1947		
new york	columbia so	45: philips A409 022E
22-23		lp: columbia (usa) ML 5113
march		lp: philips GBL 5551/G03543L
1956		lp: cbs 60505/61510
		cd: sony SMK 64467/SX10K 66247

j.strauss **g'schichten aus dem wienerwald, waltz**

london 18 may 1929	orchestra	78: columbia L 2334 78: columbia (usa) M 364 78: columbia (argentina) 264839 cd: dante LYS 358
edinburgh 13 september 1947	vienna philharmonic	cd: wing (japan) WCD 3-4
los angeles 7 may 1950	los angeles philharmonic	cd: as-disc AS 417
los angeles 2 july 1952	walter, piano	lp: discocorp BWS 807 cd: wing (japan) WCD 51
new york 22-23 march 1956	columbia so	lp: columbia (usa) ML 5113 lp: philips GBL 5551/GBR 6510/ G03543L/G05613R lp: cbs 60505/61510 cd: sony SMK 64467/SX10K 66247

j.strauss **kaiserwalzer**

vienna 18 october 1937	vienna philharmonic	78: hmv DB 3397 78: victor M 805 lp: turnabout THS 65066 cd: preiser 90139 cd: dg 435 3352/459 7342 cd: dante LYS 358
new york 18 april 1942	new york philharmonic	78: columbia (usa) 11854D 78: columbia (brazil) 30-5349
new york 5 july 1944	new york philharmonic	cd: as-disc AS 417
new york 22-23 march 1956	columbia so	lp: columbia (usa) ML 5113 lp: philips GBL 5551/GBR 6510/ G03543L/G05613R lp: cbs 61510 cd: sony SMK 64467/SX10K 66247

j.strauss **rosen aus dem süden, waltz**

berlin 14 february 1930	berlin philharmonic	78: columbia LX 28 78: columbia (germany) DWX 1337 78: columbia (italy) GQX 10989 78: columbia (argentina) 264836 78: columbia (usa) M 364 cd: preiser 90090 cd: dante LYS 358

wiener blut, waltz

berlin 10-11 january 1929	staatskapelle	78: columbia L 2270 78: columbia (argentina) 264837 lp: discocorp (japan) BWS 1003 cd: dante LYS 358
los angeles 2 july 1952	walter, piano	lp: discocorp BWS 807 cd: wing (japan) WCD 51
new york 22-23 march 1956	columbia so	lp: columbia (usa) ML 5113 lp: philips GBL 5551/GBR 6510 G03543L/G05613R lp: cbs 60505/61510 cd: sony SMK 64467/SX10K 66247

114
j.strauss **der zigeunerbaron, overture**

london 18 may 1929	orchestra	78: columbia L 2352 78: columbia (usa) 9083M 78: columbia (canada) 15185 78: columbia (argentina) 264835 cd: dante LYS 358
london 12 september 1938	london so	78: hmv DB 3650 78: victor M 805 cd: dante LYS 358 cd: grammofono AB 78548
new york 5 july 1944	new york philharmonic	unpublished radio broadcast
edinburgh 13 september 1947	vienna philharmonic	cd: wing (japan) WCD 3-4
los angeles 7 may 1950	los angeles philharmonic	cd: as-disc AS 417
new york 22-23 march 1956	columbia so	45: philips A409 022E lp: columbia (usa) ML 5113 lp: philips GBL 5551/G03543L lp: cbs 60505/61510 cd: sony SMK 64467/SX10K 66247

RICHARD STRAUSS (1864-1949)

don juan

london 13 june 1926	orchestra of the royal philharmonic society	78: columbia L 2067-2068 78: columbia (italy) GQX 10489-10490 78: columbia (usa) 67386-67387 cd: grammofono AB 78585 cd: history 205246/205241 *side one of this performance was recorded on 17 november 1926*
boston 21 january 1947	boston so	cd: wing (japan) WCD 58
berlin 25 september 1950	berlin philharmonic	lp: discocorp BWS 726/BWS 1007 lp: columbia (japan) OZ 7523 cd: nuova era NE 2234 cd: originals SH 836
den haag 4 june 1952	concertgebouw orchestra	lp: discocorp (japan) BWS 1022 lp: columbia (japan) OZ 7524 cd: wing (japan) WCD 26
new york 26-29 december 1952	new york philharmonic	lp: columbia (usa) ML 4650/ML 5338 lp: philips ABR 4058/GBL 5504/ G03508L cd: sony SMK 64466/SX10K 66247
new york 28 december 1952	new york philharmonic	unpublished radio broadcast *music performance research centre*
paris 12 may 1955	orchestre national	cd: venezia (japan) V 1006

strauss **gefunden (ich ging im walde so für mich hin)**

washington	schumann	lp: voce VOCE 117
2 april	walter, piano	lp: columbia (japan) OW 7225
1950		cd: wing (japan) WCD 51

der rosenkavalier, waltz sequence

berlin	berlin	78: columbia LX 60
14 february	philharmonic	78: columbia (germany) DWX 1348
1930		78: columbia (france) LFX 94
		78: columbia (usa) 67892D
		78: columbia (argentina) 264806
		lp: emi RLS 768/1C137 54095-54099
		cd: emi CDF 300 0122

der rosenkavalier, excerpt (da lieg' ich)

london	orchestra	78: columbia L 2340
18 may	andrassy	78: columbia (germany) DWX 1310
1929	mayr	78: columbia (usa) 9087M
		cd: preiser 89401/89950
		cd: pearl GEMMCDS 9925

tanz der 7 schleier/salome

berlin	berlin	78: columbia LX 39
14 february	philharmonic	78: columbia (germany) DWX 1342
1930		78: columbia (italy) GQX 10705
		78: columbia (usa) 67814D
		78: columbia (argentina) 264974
		lp: emi RLS 768/1C137 54095-54099
		cd: emi CDF 300 0122

strauss sinfonia domestica

new york 23 december 1945	new york philharmonic	cd: nypo historic broadcasts CD 5

till eulenspiegels lustige streiche

los angeles 1950	los angeles philharmonic	lp: discocorp (japan) BWS 1007 lp: columbia (japan) OZ 7524 cd: nuova era NE 2234 cd: urania URN 22.141

tod und verklärung

london 5 december 1924	orchestra of the royal philharmonic society	78: columbia L 1621-1623 78: columbia (usa) M 15
new york 25 march 1939	nbc so	cd: music and arts CD 656/CD 4656
new york 24 february 1951	nbc so	lp: discocorp (japan) BWS 1007 lp: columbia (japan) OZ 7524 cd: nuova era NE 2234
new york 28 december 1952	new york philharmonic	unpublished radio broadcast *music performance research centre*
new york 29 december 1952	new york philharmonic	lp: columbia (usa) ML 4650/ML 5338 lp: philips ABR 4058/GBL 5504/ G03508L cd: sony SMK 64466/SX10K 66247
london 15 may 1955	bbc so	unpublished radio broadcast *music performance research centre*

PIOTR TCHAIKOVSKY (1840-1893)

symphony no 5

new york	nbc so	cd: dante LYS 416
9 march		cd: eklipse (japan) T 6
1940		cd: music and arts CD 4273
		cd: grammofono AB 78525

symphony no 6 "pathétique"

berlin	staatskapelle	78: grammophon 66332-66336/
march		69771-69776
1925		lp: discocorp BWS 1004
		cd: polygram (japan) POCG 6067
		cd: wing (japan) WCD 29

symphony no 6, second movement

berlin	berlin	78: grammophon 69676
august,	philharmonic	
september		
or october		
1923		

tchaikovsky **piano concerto no 1**

new york	new york	lp: discocorp BWS 728
11 april	philharmonic	cd: as-disc AS 400
1948	horowitz	cd: music and arts CD 810
		cd: legends LGD 105
		cd: iron needle IN 1398

romeo and juliet, fantasy overture

los angeles	los angeles	cd: dante LYS 416
16 july	philharmonic	cd: grammofono AB 78532
1942		cd: music and arts CD 788/CD 4788
		cd: history 204244/205241

RALPH VAUGHAN WILLIAMS (1872-1958)

fantasia on a theme of thomas tallis

new york	new york	cd: as-disc AS 421
22 february	philharmonic	
1953		

GIUSEPPE VERDI (1813-1901)

aida, fragments

vienna	vienna	lp: ed smith EJS 574
16 september	philharmonic	cd: koch 3-1457-2
1937	vienna opera	
	chorus	
	nemeth	
	thorborg	
	mazarelli	
	sved	
	alsen	
	sung in german	

verdi **un ballo in maschera**

new york 15 january 1944	metropolitan opera orchestra and chorus milanov greer thorborg peerce warren	lp: discocorp BWS 805 cd: dante LYS 395-396 cd: 40s label FTO 31112
new york 22 april 1944	metropolitan opera orchestra and chorus milanov greer thorborg peerce warren	unpublished met broadcast
new york 8 december 1945	metropolitan opera orchestra and chorus milanov alarie harshaw peerce warren	unpublished met broadcast

122
verdi **don carlo, excerpts**

vienna	vienna	cd: koch 3-1460-2
16 december	philharmonic	*excerpts*
1936-	vienna opera	lp: ed smith EJS 334
5 january	chorus	*EJS 334 incorrectly dated*
1937	konetzni	*16 february 1937*
	nikolaidi	
	völker/	
	ardelli	
	kipnis	
	genrod	
	sung in german	

vienna	vienna	cd: koch 3-1452-2
7 november	philharmonic	*excerpts*
1937	vienna opera	lp: ed smith EJS 334
	chorus	lp: teletheater 762.3596-3597
	reining	cd: koch 3-1450-2
	tutsek	
	mazaroff	
	pierotic	
	alsen	
	sung in german,	
	except mazaroff,	
	who sings in	
	bulgarian	

verdi **la forza del destino**

new york 23 january 1943	metropolitan opera orchestra and chorus roman petina jagel tibbett pinza baccaloni	lp: ed smith EJS 211 lp: discocorp (japan) BWS 1101-1103 cd: as-disc AS 409-410 cd: naxos 811.0038-0040
new york 27 november 1943	metropolitan opera orchestra and chorus roman kaskas jagel tibbett pinza baccaloni	unpublished met broadcast *excerpts* lp: ed smith EJS 561

messa da requiem

new york 29 march 1959	metropolitan opera orchestra and chorus milanov elias bergonzi tozzi	lp: discocorp (japan) BWS 1023 cd: as-disc AS 408 *milanov withdraws after dies irae and* *is replaced by krall*

RICHARD WAGNER (1813-1883)

a faust overture

berlin august or october 1923	berlin philharmonic	78: grammophon 65955-65956
new york 8 april 1939	nbc so	cd: as-disc AS 414 cd: music and arts CD 248/CD 4273

der fliegende holländer, overture

london 17 november 1926	orchestra of the royal philharmonic society	78: columbia L 1961-1962 78: columbia (usa) M 68 cd: grammofono AB 78585 cd: iron needle IN 1309 cd: dante LYS 441-443 cd: vai audio VAIA 1059 cd: istituto discographico italiano IDIS 295-296 cd: history 205245/205241
amsterdam 15 march 1936	concertgebouw orchestra	lp: discocorp (japan) BWS 1014 cd: wing (japan) WCD 26

los angeles
20 february
1959
	columbia so	lp: columbia (usa) ML 5482/MS 6149
		lp: philips ABL 3333/SABL 114/
		    835 550AY
		lp: cbs BRG 72155/SBRG 72155/
		    78252
		cd: sony MK 42050/MBK 45638/
		    MPK 45701/SM2K 64456/
		    SX10K 66246

wagner **der fliegende holländer, excerpt (die frist ist um)**

new york 23 december 1934	new york philharmonic schorr	lp: ed smith EJS 487
amsterdam 15 march 1936	concertgebouw orchestra hotter	unpublished radio broadcast *in his memoirs hans hotter dates this* *performance as having taken place* *in 1937*

der fliegende holländer, excerpt (ach möchtest du bleicher seemann ....to end of act 2)

new york 23 december 1934	new york philharmonic manski list schorr	lp: ed smith EJS 487

fragments from a 1934 performance of der fliegende holländer conducted by walter at the vienna staatsoper may also survive

götterdämmerung, excerpt (starke scheite schichtet mir dort)

new york 23 march 1952	new york philharmonic flagstad	lp: ed smith EJS 167 lp: discocorp IGI 328/RR 531 cd: music and arts CD 838/CD 4838 cd: nypo historic broadcasts CD 6 cd: grammofono AB 78526 cd: nuova era NE 2201 cd: memories HR 4456-4457

wagner **götterdämmerung, dawn and rhine journey**

| london
7 december
1924 | orchestra of
the royal
philharmonic
society | 78: columbia L 1636
78: columbia (usa) 67084D |

| london
20 may
1927 | orchestra of
the royal
philharmonic
society | 78: columbia L 1636R
78: columbia (usa) 67084D
cd: dante LYS 441-443
cd: vai audio VAIA 1059
cd: istituto discographico italiano
    IDIS 295-296
*LYS 441-443 incorrectly quotes 78rpm
catalogue number as L 1636* |

| london
april
1932 | british so | 78: columbia LX 191
78: columbia (france) LFX 301
78: columbia (usa) 68101D
78: columbia (argentina) 264988
cd: dante LYS 441-443
cd: iron needle IN 1309
cd: grammofono AB 78585
cd: history 204245/205241 |

götterdämmerung, siegfried's funeral march

| london
may-june
1931 | british so | 78: columbia LX 156
78: columbia (france) LFX 246
78: columbia (usa) 68044D
78: columbia (canada) 15190
78: columbia (argentina) 264654
cd: dante LYS 441-443
cd: vai audio VAIA 1059 |

wagner **lohengrin, prelude**

new york 14 may 1944	new york philharmonic	cd: as-disc AS 414
los angeles 27 february 1959	columbia so	lp: columbia (usa) ML 5907/MS 6507/ M2L-290/M2S-690/Y-30667 lp: cbs BRG 72143/SBRG 72143/ 72139-72140/78252 cd: sony MK 42050/MBK 45638/ MPK 45701/SB2K 64372/ SM2K 64456/SX10K 66246

lohengrin, act 3 prelude

london 22 november 1926	orchestra of the royal philharmonic society	78: columbia L 1962 78: columbia (usa) 02959 cd: dante LYS 441-443 cd: grammofono AB 78585 cd: iron needle IN 1309 cd: vai audio VAIA 1059 cd: istituto discographico italiano IDIS 295-296 *LYS 441-443 incorrectly dated february 1927*
new york 14 may 1944	new york philharmonic	cd: as-disc AS 414

wagner **die meistersinger von nürnberg, overture**

london 16 may 1930	symphony orchestra	78: columbia DX 86 78: columbia (usa) 68023D 78: columbia (argentina) 264843 cd: dante LYS 441-443 cd: vai audio VAIA 1114 cd: history 205245/205241
new york 1946	new york philharmonic	soundtrack to the film *carnegie hall*
los angeles 4 december 1959	columbia so	lp: columbia (usa) ML 5482/ML 5887/ MS 6149/MS 6487 lp: philips ABL 3333/SABL 114/ 835 550AY lp: cbs BRG 72155/SBRG 72155/ 78252 cd: sony MK 42050/MBK 45638/ MPK 45701/SM2K 64456/ SB2K 64372/SX10K 66246

wagner die meistersinger von nürnberg, act 3 prelude

london 11 february 1925	orchestra of the royal philharmonic society	78: columbia L 1651 78: columbia (usa) 67086D
london april 1932	british so	78: columbia LX 180 78: columbia (france) LFX 292 78: columbia (usa) X 43 78: columbia (argentina) 264618 78: metronome ULX 3007 cd: dante LYS 441-443 cd: vai audio VAIA 1114 *LYS 441-443 incorrectly dated march 1932*

die meistersinger von nürnberg, dance of the apprentices and entry of the masters

london april-may 1932	british so	78: columbia LX 232 78: columbia (france) LFX 329 78: columbia (australia) LOX 180 78: columbia (usa) 68091D/X 43 cd: dante LYS 441-443 cd: vai audio VAIA 1114 *LYS 441-443 incorrectly dated march 1932*

130
wagner **parsifal, prelude**

london 25 november 1925	orchestra of the royal philharmonic society	78: columbia L 1744-1745 cd: dante LYS 441-443 cd: vai audio VAIA 1114 cd: istituto discographico italiano IDIS 295-296
london 19 may 1927	orchestra of the royal philharmonic society	78: columbia L 1744-1745 78: columbia (italy) GQX 10317-10318 78: columbia (usa) 67572-67573D cd: iron needle IN 1309 cd: grammofono AB 78585 cd: dante LYS 441-443 cd: history 205245/205241 *contrary to standard practice on the columbia label the suffix "R" after the original catalogue number, which would have denoted a re-recording after an earlier version, was not added*
los angeles 19 june 1949	los angeles philharmonic	cd: music and arts CD 838/CD 4838
new york 23 march 1950	new york philharmonic	cd: as-disc AS 422 cd: legends LGD 119
new york 28 december 1952	new york philharmonic	unpublished radio broadcast *music performance research centre*
san francisco 18 april 1954	san francisco symphony	lp: cls records RPCL 2031

los angeles
25 february
1959
	columbia so	lp: columbia (usa) ML 5482/MS 6149/
		    M2L-343/M2S-743
		lp: philips ABK 3333/SABL 114/
		    835 550AY
		lp: cbs BRG 72155/SBRG 72155/78252
		cd: sony MK 42038/MYK 44872/
		    SB2K 64372/SM2K 64456/SX10K 66246

wagner **parsifal, excerpt (vom bade kehrt der könig heim, orchestral arrangement)**

london 25 november 1925	orchestra of the royal philharmonic society	78: columbia L 1745 78: columbia (usa) M 68 cd: dante LYS 441-443 cd: istituto discographico italiano IDIS 295-296
london 19 may 1927	orchestra of the royal philharmonic society	78: columbia L 1745 78: columbia (italy) GQX 10318 78: columbia (usa) 67573D cd: iron needle IN 1309 cd: dante LYS 441-443 cd: vai audio VAIA 1114 *contrary to standard practice on the columbia label the suffix "R" after the original catalogue number, which would have denoted a re-recording after an earlier version, was not added*

parsifal, excerpt (klingsors zaubergarten und blumenmädchen, orchestral arrangement)

london 22 november 1925	orchestra of the royal philharmonic society	78: columbia L 1746-1747 78: columbia (usa) 67190-67191D cd: grammofono AB 78585 cd: iron needle IN 1309 cd: dante LYS 441-443 cd: vai audio VAIA 1059 cd: istituto discographico italiano IDIS 295-296 *LYS 441-443 incorrectly dated 20 november*

132
wagner **parsifal, karfreitagszauber**

san francisco 18 april 1954	san francisco symphony	lp: cls records RPCL 2031
los angeles 25 february 1959	columbia so	lp: columbia (usa) ML 5482/MS 6149/ M2L-343/M2S-743 lp: philips ABL 3333/SABL 114/ 835 550AY lp: cbs BRG 72155/SBRG 72155/ 78209/78252 cd: sony MK 42038/MYK 44872/ SB2K 64372/SM2K 64456/ SX10K 66246

rienzi, overture

london 15 june 1926	orchestra of the royal philharmonic society	78: columbia L 1820-1821 78: columbia (italy) GQX 10355-10356 78: columbia (usa) 9063-9064M cd: iron needle IN 1309 cd: dante LYS 441-443 cd: vai audio VAIA 1114 cd: istituto discographico italiano IDIS 295-296 cd: history 205245/205241 *history dated 15 november 1926*

wagner **siegfried idyll**

london 3-5 december 1924	orchestra of the royal philharmonic society	78: columbia L 1653-1654 78: columbia (usa) 67099-67100D cd: istituto discographico italiano IDIS 295-296
london 19 november 1926	orchestra of the royal philharmonic society	78: columbia L 1653-1654 78: columbia (usa) M 68/67317-67318D cd: dante LYS 441-443 *contrary to standard practice on the* *columbia label the suffix "R" after the* *original catalogue number, which would* *have denoted a re-recording after an* *earlier version, was not added*
london 16 may 1930	symphony orchestra	78: columbia LX 79-80 78: columbia (france) LFX 145-146 78: columbia (usa) X 26 78: columbia (argentina) 264286-264287 cd: dante LYS 441-443
vienna 19 june 1935	vienna philharmonic	78: hmv DB 2634-2635 78: victor G 21 lp: world records SH 193-194 lp: turnabout THS 65163 cd: emi CDH 764 2982/CHS 764 2942 cd: preiser 90157 cd: palladio PD 4169 cd: grammofono AB 78546 cd: dante LYS 441-443 cd: history 205245/205241
boston 21 january 1947	boston so	cd: wing (japan) WCD 58 *this may originate from a us forces v-disc*

134
wagner siegfried idyll/concluded

los angeles 19 june 1949	los angeles philharmonic	cd: as-disc AS 422 cd: music and arts CD 838/CD 4838 *as-disc is dated 1950*
new york 28 december 1952	new york philharmonic	unpublished radio broadcast *music performance research centre*
new york 5 january 1953	new york philharmonic	45: philips ABE 10199 lp: columbia (usa) ML 5338 lp: philips GBL 5504/G03508L
paris 5 may 1955	orchestre national	cd: venezia (japan) V 1006
new york 17 february 1957	new york philharmonic	cd: wing (japan) WCD 27 cd: legends LGD 119

los angeles
27 february
1959
	columbia so	lp: columbia (usa) ML 5907/MS 6507/
		    M2L-290/M2S-690/Y-30667
		lp: cbs BRG 72143/SBRG 72143/
		    72139-72140/78252/61128
		cd: sony MK 42036/MPK 45701/
		    SB2K 64372/SM2K 64456
		    SX10K 66246
		SM2K 64456 also includes rehearsal extracts

wagner **tannhäuser, overture and venusberg music**

los angeles	columbia so	lp: columbia (usa) ML 5907/MS 6507/
24-27	occidental	M2L-273/M2S-622/Y-30667
march	college	lp: cbs BRG 72143/SBRG 72143/
1961	concert choir	72011-72012/78252
		cd: cbs MK 42050/MBK 45638/
		MPK 45701/SB2K 64372/
		SM2K 64456/SX10K 66246

tannhäuser, venusberg music

london	orchestra of	78: columbia L 1982-1983
14 june	the royal	78: columbia (italy) GQX 10465-10466
1926	philharmonic	78: columbia (usa) M 68
	society	cd: grammofono AB 78595
		cd: iron needle IN 1309
		cd: vai audio VAIA 1114
		cd: dante LYS 441-443
		cd: istituto discographico italiano
		IDIS 295-296

tristan und isolde, prelude and liebestod

new york	new york	cd: as-disc AS 414
14 may	philharmonic	cd: music and arts CD 838/CD 4838
1944		cd: palladio PD 4217
		orchestral version of the liebestod; palladio contains prelude only

los angeles	los angeles	cd: as-disc AS 422
1950	philharmonic	cd: legends LGD 119
	harshaw	cd: historic performers HP 27
		historic performers incorrectly dated 1952

tristan und isolde, liebestod in orchestral version

london	orchestra of	78: columbia L 1652
11 february	the royal	78: columbia (usa) 67163D
1925	philharmonic	cd: grammofono AB 78585
	society	cd: vai audio VAIA 1114
		cd: dante LYS 441-443
		cd: istituto discographico italiano
		IDIS 295-296

136
wagner **die walküre, act one**

vienna	vienna	78: hmv DB 2636-2643/
20-22	philarmonic	DB 8039-8046 auto
june	lehmann	78: columbia (germany) LWX 105-112
1935	melchior	78: columbia (italy) GQX 10889-10890
	list	78: victor M 298

45: victor WCT 58
lp: hmv COLH 133
lp: hmv (france) FALP 50013
lp: electrola E 80686-80688
lp: victor LVT 1003/LCT 1033
lp: angel 60190
lp: emi 2C051 03023/1C149 03023M/
 29 01313
lp: danacord DACO 171-176
cd: danacord DACOCD 317-318
cd: emi CDH 761 0202
cd: arkadia 78526
excerpts
78: victor M 329/M 633
45: victor WCT 2
lp: victor LCT 1/LCT 1001
lp: top classic TC 9049
lp: emi 1C147 01259-01260M/
 1C147 30636-30637M/
 1C149 29116-29117M

wagner **die walküre, act two scenes 3 and 5**
vienna	vienna	78: hmv DB 3724-3725 and 3728
20-22	philharmonic	78: victor M 582
june	lehmann	lp: electrola E 80686-80688
1935	flesch	lp: turnabout THS 65163
	melchior	lp: emi 29 02123
	list	lp: danacord DACO 171-176
	jerger	cd: danacord DACOCD 317-318
		cd: emi CDH 764 2552
		excerpts
		lp: emi RLS 7711/EX 29 01313/ 1C137 54390-54396M

these scenes were added to recordings made in berlin in 1938 under the conductot seidler-winkler to constitute a completed edition of act two

die walküre, fragmentary excerpts
vienna	vienna	cd: koch 3-1459-2
13 october	philharmonic	
1936	merker	
	konetzni	
	thorborg	
	völker	
	hofmann	
	alsen	

wesendonk-lieder
new york	flagstad	lp: discocorp DIS 3700/RR 531
23 march	walter, piano	cd: as-disc AS 422
1952		cd: music and arts CD 838/CD 4838
		cd: legends LGD 119
		cd: simax PSC 1824

DIS 3700 was incorrectly dated 1944

CARL MARIA VON WEBER (1786-1826)

konzertstück for piano and orchestra

los angeles	los angeles	cd: as-disc AS 412
21 may	philharmonic	cd: eklipse EKR 1402
1950	carter	cd: history 205242/205241
		cd: urania awaiting publication

aufforderung zum tanz

los angeles	los angeles	cd: as-disc AS 412
21 may	philharmonic	cd: eklipse EKR 1402
1950		cd: urania awaiting publication

euryanthe, overture

new york	new york	cd: wing (japan) WCD 36
22 february	philharmonic	
1948		

munich	bavarian state	cd: as-disc AS 423
2 october	orchestra	cd: legends LGD 114
1950		cd: urania awaiting publication

weber **der freischütz, overture**

london 7 december 1924	orchestra of the royal philharmonic society	78: columbia (usa) 67082D cd: istituto discographico italiano IDIS 295-296
paris 9 may 1938	conservatoire orchestra	78: hmv DB 3554 lp: discocorp (japan) BWS 1006
los angeles 21 may 1950	los angeles philharmonic	cd: as-disc AS 423 cd: eklipse EKR 1402 cd: legends LGD 114 cd: history 205242/205241 *LGD 114 incorrectly dated 1958; also issued in japan by king but dated 2 may 1950*

oberon, overture

berlin 1931	berlin philharmonic	dvd: dreamlife (japan) DLVC 1009
new york 18 march 1939	nbc so	cd: music and arts CD 248/CD 4273
los angeles 19 june 1949 1950	los angeles philharmonic	cd: music and arts CD 838 cd: eklipse EKR 1402 cd: history 205242/205241 cd: urania awaiting publication
san francisco 18 april 1954	san francisco symphony	lp: cls records RPCL 2031 cd: as-disc AS 423 cd: legends LGD 114

HUGO WOLF (1860-1903)

lieder: phänomen; anakreons grab; als ich auf dem euphrat schiffte; blumengruss; in dem schatten meiner locken

washington	schumann	lp: voce records VOCE 117
2 april	walter, piano	lp: columbia (japan) OW 7225
1950		cd: wing (japan) WCD 51

Programme

Overture: "Euryanthe" - - - - Weber

Symphony No. 40 in G minor (K. 550)   Mozart
    Allegro molto
    Andante
    Menuetto: Allegretto
    Allegro assai

INTERVAL

Symphony No. 9 in C major (The Great)   Schubert
    Andante — Allegro ma non troppo
    Andante con moto
    Scherzo: Allegro vivace
    Finale: Allegro vivace

vienna philharmonic concert with walter in london (royal albert hall) on 6 october 1949

erich leinsdorf
1912-1993

BELA BARTOK (1881-1945)

concerto for orchestra

boston 13-14 october 1962	boston so	lp: victor LM 2643/LSC 2643/ RB 6536/SB 6536 cd: rca/bmg 09026 633092/74321 179072
zwolle 16 june 1965	concertgebouw orchestra	unpublished radio broadcast

violin concerto no 2

boston 23-24 april 1964	boston so silverstein	lp: victor LM 2852/LSC 2852

LUDWIG VAN BEETHOVEN (1770-1827)

symphony no 1

boston   boston so   lp: victor LSC 3098/GL 42218/
23 april   GL 42286
1969   cd: rca/bmg 09026 601282/
                                       09026 617202/74321 292392/
                                       74321 303652

symphony no 2

boston   boston so   lp: victor LSC 3032/CML 006/
6 march   GL 42218/GL 42286
1967   cd: rca/bmg VD 60130/09026 601302/
                                       74321 178892/74321 303652

symphony no 3 "eroica"

rochester   rochester   lp: columbia (usa) RL 3069/7053/
2 april   philharmonic   OK 5016
1953   lp: philips G06702R

boston   boston so   lp: victor LM 2644/LSC 2644/
30 september   RB 6560/SB 6560/GL 11525/
1962   GL 42286
                                   cd: rca/bmg RV 78782/09026 607862/
                                       09026 617132/74321 212792/
                                       74321 241992/74321 303652

leinsdorf 147

beethoven **symphony no 4**

boston 20-22 december 1966	boston so	lp:	victor LM 3006/LSC 3006/ VIC 1566/VICS 1566/GL 42219/ GL 42286
		cd:	rca/bmg RV 77452/74321 241992/ 74321 303652

symphony no 5

new york 1953	american artists' orchestra	lp:	grand award (usa) GA 33-319
boston 23 december 1967	boston so	lp:	victor LSC 7055/GL 42219/ GL 42286
		cd:	rca/bmg RV 77452/74321 241992/ 74321 303652

recording completed on 8 april 1968

symphony no 6 "pastoral"

boston 13 january 1969	boston so	lp:	victor LSC 3074/GL 42286/ GL 47501
		cd:	rca/bmg RV 79962/09026 617202/ 74321 178892/74321 303652

symphony no 7

rochester 21 march 1955	rochester philharmonic	lp:	columbia (usa) RL 6622/7074/ OK 5007
		lp:	philips G05600R/G06629R
boston 21 november 1966	boston so	lp:	victor LM 2969/LSC 2969/ RB 6733/SB 6733/GL 42222/ GL 42286
		cd:	rca/bmg RV 79972/09026 292392/ 74321 178892/74321 303652

beethoven **symphony no 8**

boston 23 april 1969	boston so	lp: victor LSC 3098/GL 42222/ GL 42286 cd: rca/bmg VD 60128/09026 601282/ 74321 212792/74321 303652

symphony no 9 "choral"

boston 21-22 april 1969	boston so pro musica and new england choirs marsh veasey domingo milnes	lp: victor LSC 7055/LSC 20130/ GL 42286 cd: rca/bmg VD 87880/RV 78822/ 09026 636822/74321 212802/ 74321 303652

piano concerto no 1

boston 20-21 october 1967	boston so rubinstein	lp: victor LSC 3013/LMDS 6417/ SRS 3006/SER 5614-5617 cd: rca/bmg RD 85674/09026 680832/ 09026 630572/09026 630002

beethoven **piano concerto no 2**

boston
21 december
1967
	boston so
	rubinstein
		lp: victor LM 2947/LSC 2947/
		    LMDS 6417/SRS 3006/SER 5614-5617/
		    ARL1-4349
		cd: rca/bmg RD 85675/09026 630592/
		    09026 630002

piano concerto no 3

boston
5-6
june
1965
	boston so
	rubinstein
		lp: victor LM 2947/LSC 2947/
		    LMDS 6417/SRS 3006/SER 5614-5617/
		    RB 6787/SB 6787
		cd: rca/bmg RD 85675/09026 630572/
		    09026 630002

piano concerto no 4

boston
20 april
1964
	boston so
	rubinstein
		lp: victor LM 2848/LSC 2848/
		    LMDS 6417/SRS 3006/SER 5614-5617/
		    RB 6787/SB 6787/AGL1-4349
		cd: rca/bmg RD 85676/09026 630582/
		    09026 630002

piano concerto no 5 "emperor"

boston
4 april
1963
	boston so
	rubinstein
		lp: victor LM 2733/LSC 6733/
		    LMDS 6417/SRS 3006/SER 5614-5617/
		    RB 6598/SB 6598/AGL1-4220/
		    CRL3-0725/VL 89029/SHZT 549
		cd: rca/bmg RD 85676/09026 630582/
		    09026 630002

zwolle 16 june 1965	concertgebouw orchestra ashkenazy	unpublished radio broadcast

150
beethoven **violin concerto**

london	philharmonia	lp: columbia 33CX 1863/SAX 2508
23-26	milstein	lp: columbia (germany) K 80314
june		lp: world records T 597/ST 597
1961		

violin concerto, abridged version of third movement

new york	rca victor	78: victor M 1428
3-4	orchestra	45: victor WDM 1428
april	mischakoff	lp: victor LM 1101
1950		*recorded for an album entitled heart of the violin concerto*

romance no 2 for violin and orchestra

brent	new	victor unpublished
14-16	philharmonia	
august	fodor	
1974		

coriolan, overture

boston	boston so	lp: victor LM 2969/LSC 2969/
21 november		RB 6733/SB 6733
1966		cd: rca/bmg RV 79972

fidelio, excerpt (gott welch' dunkel hier!)

| new york | orchestra | 78: columbia (usa) 71410D |
| 1940 | maison | |

beethoven **die geschöpfe des prometheus, overture, pastorale and finale**

boston 30 october 1967	boston so	lp: victor LSC 3032 cd: rca/bmg VD 60130 *overture only* cd: rca/bmg 09026 601302/09026 607862

leonore no 2, overture

boston 22 december 1966	boston so	lp: victor LM 3006/LSC 3006/ VIC 1566/VICS 1566

leonore no 3, overture

london 24 may 1958	philharmonia	lp: capitol P 8465/SP 8465
boston 6 january 1963	boston so	lp: victor LM 2701/LSC 2701/ RB 6582/SB 6582/OPO 1002

unspecified german dances by beethoven recorded by leinsdorf with london so in london on 7-8 march 1975 by cbs but remain unpublished

ALBAN BERG (1885-1935)

der wein, concert aria
boston	boston so	lp: victor LSC 7044/LMDS 7044/
19 april	curtin	RE 5542-5543/SER 5542-5543
1965		

wozzeck, three fragments
boston	boston so	lp: victor LM 7031/LSC 7031/LMDS 7031/
23 april	sacred heart	RE 5518-5519/SER 5518-5519
1964	choir	
	curtin	

HECTOR BERLIOZ (1803-1869)

marche hongroise/la damnation de faust
boston	boston so	lp: victor LM 2757/LSC 2757
8-13		
april		
1964		

GEORGES BIZET (1838-1875)

carmen, abridged version on twelve 78rpm sides
new york	rca victor	78: victor M 1078
22-31	orchestra	78: hmv DB 6566-6571
may	and chorus	lp: victor LM 1007
1946	swarthout	*excerpts*
	albanese	78: victor 14419/11-9794/12-0014
	vinay	lp: victor LM 111/LM 115/LM 1156
	merrill	cd: preiser 89501
		cd: pearl GEMM 0064

JOHANNES BRAHMS (1833-1897)

symphony no 1

philadelphia 16 july 1952	robin hood dell orchestra	45: victor WBC 1004 lp: victor LBC 1004
boston 29 september 1963	boston so	lp: victor LM 2711/LSC 2711

symphony no 2

boston 16-18 december 1964	boston so	lp: victor LM 2809/LSC 2809/ALK1-4482 cd: rca/bmg VD 60129/09026 680822

symphony no 3

london 23-24 may 1958	philharmonia	lp: capitol P 8483/SP 8483 lp: pickwick (usa) PC 4007/SPC 4007 lp: world records (australia) STE 270 cd: emi CDM 565 6122/CDM 567 0212 *pickwick issue incorrectly describes* *orchestra as los angeles philharmonic*
boston 7 march 1966	boston so	lp: victor LM 2936/LSC 2936/ RB 6725/SB 6725

brahms **symphony no 4**

prague 1966	czech po	cd: multisonic 310.0232
boston 26-27 april 1966	boston so	lp: victor

piano concerto no 1

boston 16-18 march 1964	boston so cliburn	lp: victor LM 2724/LSC 2724/ RB 6586/SB 6586 cd: rca/bmg GD 60357/09026 603572
boston 21-22 april 1964	boston so rubinstein	lp: victor LM 2971/LSC 2917/VCS 7071 RB 6726/SB 6726 cd: rca/bmg 09026 630592/09026 630002
chicago 19 november 1979	chicago so berman	lp: cbs 35850 cd: oony MYK 44714

piano concerto no 2

chicago 17-18 october 1960	chicago so richter	lp: victor LM 2466/LSC 2466/RB 16235/ SB 2106/VIC 1563/VICS 1563/ GL 11267/AGL1-1267 lp: melodiya D018867-018868 cd: rca/bmg GD 86518/07863 565182

violin concerto, abridged version of third movement

new york 3-4 april 1950	rca victor orchestra mischakoff	78: victor M 1428 45: victor WDM 1428 lp: victor LM 1101 *recorded for an album entitled heart of the violin concerto*

1971 performance of the complete concerto by szeryng and czech philhatmonic conducted by zecchi and issued on praga cd PR 250081 is described by gramophone catalogue 1999 as conducted by leinsdorf

brahms **haydn variations**

london	philharmonia	lp: capitol P 8483/SP 8483
21-23		lp: pickwick (usa) PC 4007/SPC 4007
may		lp: world records (australia) STE 270
1958		*pickwick issue incorrectly describes orchestra as los angeles philharmonic*

tragic overture

boston	boston so	lp: victor LM 2936/LSC 2936/
26 april		RB 6725/SB 6725
1966		

es ist ein ros entsprungen, chorale prelude arranged by leinsdorf

cleveland	cleveland	78: columbia (usa) M 617
25 february	orchestra	
1946		

o gott du frommer gott, chorale prelude arranged by leinsdorf

cleveland	cleveland	78: columbia (usa) M 834
15 august	orchestra	
1946		

brahms **ein deutsches requiem**

boston	boston so	lp: victor LSC 7054/SB 6825
25 november-	new england	cd: rca/bmg GD 86800
16 december	chorus	*recording completed on 17 february 1969*
1968	caballé	
	milnes	

vier ernste gesänge

boston	milnes	lp: victor LSC 7054/SB 6825
22-23	leinsdorf, piano	
january		
1969		

piano quartet in g minor, orchestral arrangement by schoenberg

berlin	berlin	cd: faschmann klassik CDR 59
26-27	philharmonic	
june		
1983		

unspecified hungarian dances by brahms recorded by leinsdorf and london so by cbs in london on 7 march 1975 but remain unpublished

ANTON BRUCKNER (1824-1896)

symphony no 4 "romantic"
boston   boston so   lp: victor LM 2915/LSC 2915/
10-11   RB 6697/SB 6697
january
1966

MAX BRUCH (1838-1920)

violin concerto no 1, abridged version of first movement
new york   rca victor   78: victor M 1428
3-4   orchestra   45: victor WDM 1428
april   mischakoff   lp: victor LM 1101
1950   *recorded for an album entitled heart of the violin concerto*

FERRUCCIO BUSONI (1866-1924)

fragments from doktor faust
berlin   berlin   unpublished radio broadcast
26-27   philharmonic
june   fischer-dieskau
1983

ELLIOTT CARTER (born 1908)

piano concerto
boston   boston so   lp: victor LM 3001/LSC 3001/
6-7   lateiner   RB 6756/SB 6756
january
1967

EMANUEL CHABRIER (1841-1894)

espana, rapsodie pour orchestre
los angeles   concert arts   lp: capitol P 8446/SP 8446
3-7   orchestra   cd: emi CDM 565 2052
march
1958

MICHAEL COLGRASS (born 1932)

as quiet as do

boston 19 april 1967	boston so	lp: victor LM 3001/LSC 3001/ RB 6756/SB 6756

AARON COPLAND (1900-1990)

music for the theatre

new york 2 march 1985	new york philharmonic	cd: new york philharmonic NYPO 9904

PETER CORNELIUS (1824-1874)

der barbier von bagdad

london 11-15 may 1956	philharmonia and chorus schwarzkopf hoffman gedda unger wächter prey	lp: columbia 33CX 1400-1401 lp: columbia (germany) C 90885-90886/ 33WCX 1400-1401 lp: angel 3553 lp: regal zonophone RZG 2047-2048 cd: emi CMS 565 2842

CLAUDE DEBUSSY (1862-1918)

la mer
los angeles 16-18 march 1957	los angeles philharmonic	lp: capitol P 8395/SP 8395 cd: emi CDM 565 4252

prélude a l'apres-midi d'un faune
los angeles 16-18 march 1957	los angeles philharmonic	lp: capitol P 8395/SP 8395
culver city 29 april 1985	los angeles philharmoniv	lp: sheffield lab SLS 10043 cd: sheffield lab LAB 24

pelléas et mélisande, orchestral suite arranged by leinsdorf
cleveland 22-24 february 1946	cleveland orchestra	78: columbia (usa) M 845 lp: columbia (usa) ML 4090 cd: cleveland orchestra TC093-75
chicago 26-29 november 1986	chicago so	cd: chicago symphony orchestra CD 0008

GAETONO DONIZETTI (1797-1848)

lucia di lammermoor
rome august- september 1957	rome opera orchestra and chorus peters peerce tozzi maero	lp: victor LM 6055/LSC 6141/ RB 16056-16057/VIC 6101/ VICS 6101/VL 43538 cd: rca/bmg 09026 685372

PAUL DUKAS (1865-1935)

l' apprenti sorcier

los angeles 3-7 march 1958	concert arts orchestra	lp: capitol P 8446/SP 8446

HENRI DUPARC (1848-1933)

mélodies: l'invitation au voyage; phidylé

new york 24 may 1949	rca victor orchestra maynor	78: victor 12-1251 45: victor 49-1279

ANTONIN DVORAK (1841-1904)

symphony no 6
cleveland 22 february 1946	cleveland orchestra	78: columbia (usa) M 687 lp: columbia (usa) ML 4269/P 14159
boston 19-22 december 1967	boston so	lp: victor LM 3017/LSC 3017

symphony no 9 "from the new world"
los angeles 10 march 1958	los angeles philharmonic	lp: capitol P 8454/SP 8454 cd: emi CDM 565 6122

romance for violin and orchestra
boston 18-19 december 1967	boston so perlman	lp: victor LSC 3014/SB 6768/VICS 2000 cd: rca/bmg 09026 635912

slavonic dances nos 2 and 8
boston 22-23 december 1967	boston so	lp: victor LM 3017/LSC 3017

russalka, excerpt (o silver moon!)
new york 24 may 1949	rca victor orchestra maynor *sung in english*	78: victor 12-1078

songs: maiden's lament; tune the strings!
new york 24 may 1949	rca victor orchestra maynor *sung in english*	78: victor 12-1078

unspecified slavonic dances recorded by leinsdorf and london so in london on 7-8 march 1975 for cbs but remain unpublished

GABRIEL FAURE (1845-1924)

élégie for cello and orchestra
boston   boston so   lp: victor LM 2703/LSC 2703/
23 march   mayes   RB 6581/SB 6581
1963

IRVING FINE (1914-1962)

toccata concertante
boston   boston so   lp: victor LM 2829/LSC 2829
25 january   cd: phoenix PHCD 106
1965

serious song
boston   boston so   lp: victor LM 2829/LSC 2829
25 january   cd: phoenix PHCD 106
1965   *recording completed on 10 january 1966*

CESAR FRANCK (1822-1890)

symphony in d minor
philadelphia   robin hood   45: victor WBC 1001
18 july   dell orchestra   lp: victor LBC 1001
1952

variations symphoniques pour piano et orchestre
london   london so   lp: columbia (usa) M 33072
20-21   watts
may
1974

ALBERTO GINASTERA (1916-1983)

piano concerto

boston 6 march 1968	boston so martins	lp: victor LM 3029/LSC 3029/ RB 6784/SB 6784

variaciones concertantes for piano and orchestra

boston 11 march 1968	boston so martins	lp: victor LM 3029/LSC 3029/ RB 6784/SB 6784

CHRISTOPH WILLIBALD GLUCK (1714-1787)

orfeo ed euridice

new york 20 january 1940	metropolitan opera orchestra and chorus thorborg novotna farell dickey	cd: walhall WHL 32

CHARLES GOUNOD (1818-1893)

roméo et juliette, excerpt (je veux vivre dans cette reve)

new york 18 august 1941	columbia so sayao	78: columbia (usa) 17301D cd: sony MHK 62355

EDVARD GRIEG (1843-1907)

piano concerto

philadelphia 8 july 1953	robin hood dell orchestra dorfman	45: victor WBC 1043 lp: victor LBC 1043/LM 2102 *also issued on victor lps in france and italy*
los angeles 4 september 1957	los angeles philharmonic pennario	lp: capitol P 8441/SP 8441 *recording completed on 22 september 1957*

peer gynt, suite no 1

rochester 20 march 1955	rochester philharmonic	lp: columbia (usa) HL 7057/OK 5005

FRANZ JOSEF HAYDN (1732-1809)

symphony no 45 "farewell"
new york	american	lp: grand award (usa) GA 33-301/GA 33-319
1953	artists'	lp: pilotone (usa) DA 302
	orchestra	*spoken commentary by deems taylor*

symphony no 93
boston	boston so	lp: victor LM 3030/LSC 3030/
19 december		VIC 1577/VICS 1577
1966		

symphony no 94 "surprise"
rochester	rochester	lp: columbia (usa) RL 6621/HL 7105
20 march	philharmonic	
1955		

symphony no 96 "miracle"
boston	boston so	lp: victor LM 3030/LSC 3030/
8 april		VIC 1577/VICS 1577
1968		

symphony no 101 "clock"
rochester	rochester	lp: columbia (usa) RL 6621/HL 7171
21 march	philharmonic	
1955		

LEOS JANACEK (1854-1928)

cunning little vixen, suite from the opera
boston	boston so	cd: boston symphony orchestra
30 september		centennial edition
1966		

NORMAN DELLO JOIO (born 1913)

fantasy and variations for piano and orchestra
boston   boston so   lp: victor LM 2667/LSC 2667/
17 february   hollander   RB 6546/SB 6546
1963

PIET KETTING (1904-1984)

due canzoni
amsterdam   concertgebouw   lp: donemus DAVS 7002
11 january   orchestra
1970

ZOLTAN KODALY (1882-1967)

hary janos, suite
london   philharmonia   lp: capitol P 8508/SP 8508
20-27   lp: angel 60209
may   cd: emi CDM 565 9232
1958

boston   boston so   lp: victor RB 6663/SB 6663/GL 42698
22 april   cd: rca/bmg 74321 179072
1965

peacock variations
boston   boston so   lp: victor RB 6663/SB 6663
23 november   cd: rca/bmg 09026 633092
1964

ERICH WOLFGANG KORNGOLD (1897-1957)

die tote stadt
munich	munich radio	lp: victor ARL3-1199
june	orchestra	cd: rca/bmg GD 87767
1975	bavarian	
	radio chorus	
	neblett, kollo	
	prey, luxon	

EDOUARD LALO (1823-1892)

symphonie espagnole for violin and orchestra
boston	boston so	lp: victor LSC 3014/SB 6768
3 september	perlman	cd: rca/bmg GD 86520/09026 683382
1968		

symphonie espagnole for violin and orchestra, second movement
new york	rca victor	78: victor M 1428
3-4	orchestra	45: victor WDM 1428
april	mischakoff	lp: victor LM 1101
1950		*recorded for an album entitled heart of the violin concerto*

LANDRE

permutazioni sinfoniche
zwolle	concertgebouw	unpublished radio broadcast
16 june	orchestra	
1965		

JOSEPH LANNER (1801-1843)

mozartisten-walzer
boston	boston so	cd: boston symphony orchestra
undated		centennial edition

FRANZ LISZT (1811-1886)

totentanz for piano and orchestra
london	london so	lp: columbia (usa) M 33072
20-21	watts	lp: cbs 60271
may		cd: sony MPT 38778
1974		cd: philips 456 9852

GUSTAV MAHLER (1860-1911)

symphony no 1

boston 20-21 october 1962	boston so	lp: victor LM 2642/LSC 2642/RB 6526/ SB 6526/VICS 2027/GL 12941/GL 42294 cd: rca/bmg 09026 634692/74321 178962
london 19-20 april 1971	royal philharmonic	lp: decca PFS 4232/SPA 521/VIV 57 lp: london (usa) SPC 21068

symphony no 3

boston 10-11 october 1966	boston so new england chorus verrett	lp: victor LSC 7046/SB 6765-6766 cd: rca/bmg 09026 634692
berlin 13 september 1984	berlin philharmonic saint hedwig's choir wenkel	cd: faschmann klassik CDR 59

mahler **symphony no 4**

amsterdam	concertgebouw	unpublished radio broadcast
9 july	orchestra	
1960	stader	

symphony no 5

boston	boston so	lp: victor LM 7031/LSC 7031/LMDS 7031/
17-26		RE 5518-5519/SER 5518-5519
november		cd: rca/bmg VD 60482/74321 292492
1963		

symphony no 6

boston	boston so	lp: victor LM 7044/LSC 7044/LMDS 7044/
20-21		RE 5542-5543/SER 5542-5543
april		
1965		

symphony no 6, first movement rehearsal extract

munich	bavarian radio	cd: bavarian radio orchestra RO 49-99
june	orchestra	
1983		

ich atmet' einen linden duft/rückert-lieder

amsterdam	concertgebouw	unpublished radio broadcast
9 july	orchestra	*other rückert-lieder also performed*
1960	stader	

JULES MASSENET (1842-1912)

manon, excerpt (je marche sur tous les chemins)

new york	columbia so	78: columbia (usa) 17301D
18 august	sayao	cd: sony MHK 62355
1941		

FELIX MENDELSSOHN-BARTHOLDY (1809-1847)

symphony no 4 "italian"

rochester 24 march 1954	rochester philharmonic	lp: columbia (usa) RL 3102/HL 7171

piano concerto no 1

philadelphia 8 july 1953	robin hood dell orchestra dorfman	45: victor WBC 1043 lp: victor LBC 1043/LM 2102 *also issued on victor lps in france and italy*

violin concerto, abridged version of first movement

new york 3-4 april 1950	rca victor orchestra mischakoff	78: victor M 1428 45: victor WDM 1428 lp: victor LM 1101 *recorded for an album entitled heart of the violin concerto*

a midsummer night's dream, incidental music

boston
29-30
november
1962
	boston so
	and chorus
	saunders
	vanni
	swenson,
	narrator
		lp: victor LM 2673/LSC 2673/RB 6557/
		    SB 6557/VL 84483
		cd: rca/bmg RV 78162/09026 609102/
		    74321 242032/74321 404602
		recording completed on 10 january 1963;
		74321 404602 omits spoken narration

a midsummer night's dream, nocturne

new york 1953	silvertone so	lp: silvertone (usa) 19 lp: mercury (usa) MG 10021

GIAN CARLO MENOTTI (born 1911)

the death of the bishop of brindisi

boston	boston so	lp: victor LM 2785/LSC 2785/
19 october	conservatory	RB 6609/SB 6609
1964	choir	
	london	

WOLFGANG AMADEUS MOZART (1756-1791)

symphony no 1

walthamstow   royal   lp: westminster XWN 18861/P 296
11-27   philharmonic   lp: emi XLP 20093/SXLP 20093
july   cd: mca classics MCAD 29808
1956

symphony no 2

walthamstow   royal   lp: westminster XWN 18861/P 296
11-27   philharmonic   lp: emi XLP 20093/SXLP 20093
july   cd: mca classics MCAD 29808
1956

symphony no 3

walthamstow   royal   lp: westminster XWN 18861/P 296
11-27   philharmonic   lp: emi XLP 20093/SXLP 20093
july   cd: mca classics MCAD 29808
1956

symphony no 4

walthamstow   royal   lp: westminster XWN 18861/P 296
11-27   philharmonic   lp: emi XLP 20093/SXLP 20093
july   cd: mca classics MCAD 29808
1956

symphony no 5

walthamstow   royal   lp: westminster XWN 18861/P 296
11-27   philharmonic   lp: emi XLP 20093/SXLP 20093
july   cd: mca classics MCAD 29808
1956

orchestra described for these westminster mozart sessions as philharmonic symphony orchestra

mozart **symphony no 6**

walthamstow	royal	lp: westminster XWN 18862/P 296/
1956	philharmonic	MS 181/W 14093
		cd: mca classics MCAD 29808

symphony no 7

walthamstow	royal	lp: westminster XWN 18862/P 297/
1956	philharmonic	MS 181/W 14093
		cd: mca classics MCAD 29808

symphony no 8

walthamstow	royal	lp: westminster XWN 18862/P 297/
1956	philharmonic	MS 181/W 14093
		cd: mca classics MCAD 29808

symphony no 9

walthamstow	royal	lp: westminster XWN 18862/P 297/
1956	philharmonic	MS 181/W 14093
		cd: mca classics MCAD 29808

orchestra described for these westminster mozart sessions as philharmonic symphony orchestra

mozart **symphony no 10**

walthamstow   royal   lp: westminster XWN 18863/P 297
11-27   philharmonic   cd: mca classics MCAD 29808
july
1956

symphony no 11

walthamstow   royal   lp: westminster XWN 18863/P 297
11-27   philharmonic   cd: mca classics MCAD 29808
july
1956

symphony no 12

walthamstow   royal   lp: westminster XWN 18863/P 297
11-27   philharmonic   cd: mca classics MCAD 29808
july
1956

symphony no 13

walthamstow   royal   lp: westminster XWN 18863/P 298
11-27   philharmonic   cd: mca classics MCAD 29808
july
1956

symphony no 14

walthamstow   royal   lp: westminster XWN 18864/P 298/
11-27   philharmonic   WST 14078
july   cd: mca classics MCAD 29808
1956

symphony no 15

walthamstow   royal   lp: westminster XWN 18864/P 298/
11-27   philharmonic   WST 14078
july   cd: mca classics MCAD 29808
1956

orchestra described for these westminster mozart sessions as philharmonic symphony orchestra

mozart **symphony no 16**

walthamstow 11-27 july 1956	royal philharmonic	lp: westminster XWN 18864/P 298/ WST 14078 cd: mca classics MCAD 29812

symphony no 17

walthamstow 11-27 july 1956	royal philharmonic	lp: westminster XWN 18864/P 298/ WST 14078 cd: mca classics MCAD 29812

symphony no 18

walthamstow 1956	royal philharmonic	lp: westminster XWN 18782/P 299/ cd: mca classics MCAD 29812

symphony no 19

walthamstow 1956	royal philharmonic	lp: westminster XWN 18782/P 299 cd: mca classics MCAD 29812

symphony no 20

walthamstow 1956	royal philharmonic	lp: westminster XWN 18782/P 299 cd: mca classics MCAD 29812

orchestra described for these westminster mozart sessions as philharmonic symphony orchestra

mozart **symphony no 21**

walthamstow	royal	lp: westminster XWN 18756/P 300
3-27	philharmonic	cd: mca classics MCAD 29812
may		
1955		

symphony no 22

walthamstow	royal	lp: westminster XWN 18756/P 300
3-27	philharmonic	cd: mca classics MCAD 29812
may		
1955		

symphony no 23

walthamstow	royal	lp: westminster XWN 18756/P 300
3-27	philharmonic	cd: mca classics MCAD 29812
may		
1955		

symphony no 24

walthamstow	royal	lp: westminster XWN 18756/P 300
3-27	philharmonic	cd: mca classics MCAD 29812
may		
1955		

symphony no 25

walthamstow	royal	lp: westminster XWN 18675/P 301
3-27	philharmonic	cd: mca classics MCAD 29812
may		
1955		

symphony no 26

walthamstow	royal	lp: westminster XWN 18675/P 301
3-27	philharmonic	cd: mca classics MCAD 29812
may		
1955		

orchestra described for these westminster mozart sessions as philharmonic symphony orchestra

mozart **symphony no 27**

walthamstow 3-27 may 1955	royal philharmonic	lp: westminster XWN 18675/P 301 cd: mca classics MCAD 29814

symphony no 28

walthamstow 3-27 may 1955	royal philharmonic	lp: westminster XWN 18675/P 301 cd: mca classics MCAD 29814

symphony no 29

walthamstow 3-27 may 1955	royal philharmonic	lp: westminster XWN 18216 cd: mca classics MCAD 29814
new york 16 january 1987	new york philharmonic	cd: new york philharmonic NYP 9701

symphony no 30

walthamstow 3-27 may 1955	royal philharmonic	lp: westminster XWN 18216 cd: mca classics MCAD 29814

orchestra for these westminster mozart sessions described as philharmonic symphony orchestra

mozart **symphony no 31 "paris"**
walthamstow	royal	lp: westminster XWN 18216
3-27	philharmonic	cd: mca classics MCAD 29814
may		
1955		

symphony no 32
walthamstow	royal	lp: westminster XWN 18216
3-27	philharmonic	cd: mca classics MCAD 29814
may		
1955		

symphony no 33
walthamstow	royal	lp: westminster XWN 18186
3-27	philharmonic	cd: mca classics MCAD 29814
may		
1955		

symphony no 34
walthamstow	royal	lp: westminster XWN 18186
3-27	philharmonic	cd: mca classics MCAD 29814
may		
1955		

minuet k409/symphony no 34
cleveland	cleveland	78: columbia (usa) 12749D
25 february	orchestra	
1946		

london	london so	lp: columbia (usa) M 35154
8 march		lp: cbs 76473
1975		cd: sony SBK 48266

symphony no 35 "haffner"
rochester	rochester	lp: columbia (usa) RL 3103/OK 5025
23 march	philharmonic	
1954		

walthamstow	royal	lp: westminster XWN 18146/P 304
3-27	philharmonic	lp: world records T 377
may		cd: mca classics MCAD 29814
1955		

orchestra for westminster mozart sessions described as philharmonic symphony orchestra

180
mozart **symphony no 36 "linz"**

walthamstow 3-27 may 1955	royal philharmonic	lp: westminster XWN 18146/P 304 lp: world records T 377 cd: mca classics MCAD 29818
boston 22 december 1967	boston so	lp: victor LM 3097/LSC 3097/VIC 1529/ VICS 1529/CCV 5050 cd: rca/bmg 09026 609072

symphony no 37, completion by michael haydn

walthamstow 3-27 may 1955	royal philharmonic	lp: westminster XWN 18146/P 304 lp: world records T 377 cd: mca classics MCAD 29818

symphony no 38 "prague"

walthamstow 3-27 may 1955	royal philharmonic	lp: westminster XWN 18116/P 305 lp: emi 1C045 90317 cd: mca classics MCAD 29818

orchestra described for westminster mozart sessions as philharmonic symphony orchestra

mozart **symphony no 39**

walthamstow 3-27 may 1955	royal philharmonic	lp: westminster XWN 18116/P 305 lp: emi 1C045 90317 cd: mca classics MCAD 29818
boston 20 january 1969	boston so	lp: victor LM 3097/LSC 3097/VIC 1529/ VICS 1529/CCV 5050 cd: rca/bmg 09026 609072 *recording completed on 23-25 april 1969*

symphony no 40

rochester 3 april 1953	rochester philharmonic	lp: columbia (usa) RL 3070/HL 7054/OK 5018
walthamstow 3-27 may 1955	royal philharmonic	lp: westminster XWN 18527/P 306 cd: mca classics MCAD 29818

symphony no 41 "jupiter"

rochester 24 march 1954	rochester philharmonic	lp: columbia (usa) RL 3103/OK 5025
walthamstow 3-27 may 1955	royal philharmonic	lp: westminster XWN 18527/P 306 cd: mca classics MCAD 29818

boston
14 january
1963
	boston so	lp: victor LM 2694/LCS 2694/RB 6567/
		    SB 6567/VIC 1485/VICS 1485/
		    VL 84484/CCV 5000
		cd: rca/bmg RD 93052

violin concerto no 3, abridged version of third movement

new york 3-4 april 1950	rca victor orchestra mischakoff	78: victor M 1428 45: victor WDM 1428 lp: victor LM 1101 *recorded for an album entitled heart of the violin concerto*

orchestra described for westminster mozart sessions as philharmonic symphony orchestra

mozart **serenade no 10 for thirteen wind**

chicago undated	chicago so members	cd: chicago symphony orchestra CD 9102

serenade no 13 "eine kleine nachtmusik"

rochester 2 april 1954	rochester philharmonic	78: columbia (usa) J 218 45: columbia (usa) J4-218 *this recording omits romanze movement*

boston
6 january
1963
	boston so	lp: victor LM 2694/LSC 2694/RB 6567/
		    SB 6567/VIC 1485/VICS 1485/
		    VL 84484/CCV 5000
		cd: rca/bmg RD 93052/09026 609072/
		    09026 681132

six german dances k509

london 8 march 1975	london so	lp: columbia (usa) M 35154 lp: cbs 76473 cd: sony SBK 48266

three marches k408

london 13 june 1975	london so	lp: columbia (usa) M 35154 lp: cbs 76473

march no 1/three marches k408

london undated	philharmonia	unpublished radio broadcast

mozart **six minuets k599**

london	london so	lp: columbia (usa) M 35154
13 june		lp: cbs 76473
1975		

requiem mass

boston	boston so	lp: victor LM 7030/LM 9982/
19 january	boston choirs	LSC 7030/LSC 9982
1964	endich	*recorded at performance in boston cathedral*
	alberts	*in memory of john f. kennedy*
	di virgilio	
	morgan	

cosi fan tutte

walthamstow	new	lp: victor LM 6416/LSC 6416/
24 august-	philharmonia	RE 5575-5578/SER 5575-5578
8 september	ambrosian	cd: rca/bmg GD 86677
1967	chorus	*excerpts*
	price	cd: rca/bmg 09026 681532
	troyanos	
	raskin	
	shirley	
	milnes	
	flagello	

cosi fan tutte, excerpt (soave sia il vento)

new york	metropolitan	lp: mrf records MRF 7/AU 487B
16 april	opera orchestra	*performed at farewell gala in old metropolitan*
1966	stratas	*opera house*
	miller	
	guarrera	
	sung in english	

mozart **don giovanni**

vienna
11-24
june
1959
	vienna
	philharmonic
	vienna opera
	chorus
	price
	nilsson
	ratti
	valletti
	siepi
	corena
		lp: victor LM 6410/LD 6410/LSC 6410/
		    LDS 6410/RE 25028-25031/
		    SER 4528-4531
		lp: decca D10 D4
		cd: decca 444 5942
		excerpts
		lp: victor LM 2847/LSC 2847/
		    RB 6654/SB 6654
		lp: decca GRV 10
		cd: decca 421 8752/440 4022/440 6542/
		    458 2452/458 3982

new york 14 january 1961	metropolitan opera orchestra and chorus steber della casa hurley gedda siepi corena	unpublished met broadcast

don giovanni, excerpts (madamina!; ah pieta signori miei!)

new york 6 february 1941	columbia so baccaloni	78: columbia (usa) 71048D

don giovanni, excerpt (batti batti!)

new york 9 march 1942	columbia so sayao	78: columbia (usa) 71577D cd: sony MHK 63221

new york 5 september 1945	rca victor orchestra steber	78: victor 11-9114

don giovanni, excerpt (vedrai carino)

new york 9 march 1942	columbia so sayao	78: columbia (usa) 71577D cd: sony MHK 63221

mozart **le nozze di figaro**

san francisco 12 october 1940	san francisco opera orchestra rethberg sayao stevens pinza brownlee	lp: ed smith EJS 301 *act two only recorded; section of finale is missing and another performance substituted*
new york 11 january 1958	metropolitan opera orchestra and chorus della casa güden miller london tozzi	unpublished met broadcast
vienna 14-25 june 1958	vienna philharmonic vienna opera chorus della casa peters elias london tozzi	lp: victor LM 6408/LSC 6408/ RE 25009-25012/SER 4508-4511 lp: decca ECS 743-745 cd: decca 444 6022 *excerpts* lp: victor LM 6079/LSC 6079
new york 23 january 1960	metropolitan opera orchestra and chorus della casa söderström miller borg siepi	unpublished met broadcast
new york 28 january 1961	metropolitan opera orchestra and chorus amara peters miller borg siepi	unpublished met broadcast

186
mozart **le nozze di figaro, overture**

london	philharmonia	lp: capitol P 8465/SP 8465
21 may		
1958		

le nozze di figaro, excerpts (non so piu; voi che sapete)

new york	columbia so	78: columbia (usa) 17298D
1941	stevens	

le nozze di figaro, excerpt (la vendetta!)

new york	columbia so	78: columbia (usa) 71193D
6 february	baccaloni	78: columbia (australia) LOX 522
1941		

le nozze di figaro, excerpts (porgi amor; dove sono)

new york	rca victor	78: victor M 1157/11-8850
22 february	orchestra	45: victor WDM 1157/49-0646
1945	steber	cd: rca/bmg GD 60521

mozart **der schauspieldirektor, overture**

new york	silvertone so	lp: silvertone (usa) 19
1953		lp: mercury (usa) MG 10021

die zauberflöte

new york	metropolitan	unpublished met broadcast
6 december	opera orchestra	
1958	and chorus	
	davy	
	peters	
	allen	
	gedda	
	uppmann	
	tozzi	
	scott	

die zauberflöte, excerpt (ach ich fühl's)

new york	rca victor	78: victor 11-9114
5 september	orchestra	cd: rca/bmg GD 60521
1945	steber	cd: metropolitan opera guild MET 517
	sung in english	

die zauberflöte, excerpt (drei knaben jung schön hold und weise)

new york	metropolitan	lp: mrf records MRF 7
16 april	opera orchestra	*performed at farewell gala in old metropolitan*
1966	pracht	*opera house*
	grillo	
	kriese	
	shirley	
	uppmann	

die zauberflöte, excerpt (marsch der priester)

london	london so	lp: columbia (usa) M 35154
march		lp: cbs 76473
1975		

MODEST MUSSORGSKY (1839-1881)

boris godunov

new york 21 march 1959	metropolitan opera orchestra and chorus roggero rankin gari kullmann siepi harvuot tozzi alvary	unpublished met broadcast
new york 7 january 1961	metropolitan opera orchestra and chorus stratas dunn sullivan kelley london borg tozzi flagello	unpublished met broadcast *main scenes of boris* cd: di stefano records GDS 2204

NICCOLO PAGANINI (1782-1840)

violin concerto no 1

brent	new	lp: victor ARL1-1565
14-16	philharmonia	
august	fodor	
1974		

AMILCARE PONCHIELLI (1834-1886)

dance of the hours/la gioconda

los angeles	concert arts	lp: capitol P 8488/SP 8488
7 march	orchestra	
1958		

SERGE PROKOFIEV (1891-1953)

symphony no 2

boston boston so lp: victor LSC 3061/SB 6794
25 march
1968

symphony no 3

boston boston so lp: victor LM 2934/LSC 2934/
25 april RB 6705/SB 6705
1966

symphony no 5

boston boston so lp: victor LM 2707/LSC 2707/
28 october RB 6576/SB 6576
1963 cd: rca/bmg 74321 212922

projected complete prokofiev symphony cycle was never completed

prokofiev **symphony no 6**

boston 23-24 april 1965	boston so	lp: victor LM 2834/LSC 2834/ RB 6662/SB 6662

piano concerto no 1

boston 1-2 december 1965	boston so browning	lp: victor LM 2897/LSC 2897/ RB 6690/SB 6690

piano concerto no 2

boston 1 december 1965	boston so browning	lp: victor LM 2897/LSC 2897/ RB 6690/SB 6690

piano concerto no 3

london 13-16 september 1960	philharmonia browning	lp: capitol P 8545/SP 8545 lp: angel 60224 cd: emi CDM 565 9232
boston 25-27 november 1967	boston so browning	lp: victor LM 3019/LSC 3019/SB 6819

prokofiev **piano concerto no 4**

boston	boston so	lp: victor LM 3019/LSC 3019/SB 6819
27 november	browning	
1967		

piano concerto no 5

boston	boston so	lp: victor LM 2732/LSC 2732/
april	hollander	RB 6597/SB 6597
1964		

boston	boston so	lp: victor LSC 3121/SB 6827
25 april	browning	
1969		

violin concerto no 1

boston	boston so	lp: victor LM 2732/LSC 2732/
13 april	friedman	RB 6597/SB 6597
1964		

violin concerto no 2

boston	boston so	lp: victor LM 2962/LSC 2962/
21 december	perlman	RB 6722/SB 6722
1966		cd: rca/bmg 09026 614542

prokofiev **sinfonia concertante for cello and orchestra**

boston 25 march 1963	boston so mayes	lp: victor LM 2703/LSC 2703/ RB 6581/SB 6581

lieutenant kijé, suite

london 21-27 may 1958	philharmonia iordachescu	lp: capitol P 8508/SP 8508 lp: angel 60209 cd: emi CDM 565 9232
boston 22 april 1968	boston so clatworthy	lp: victor LSC 3061/SB 6794/GL 42698 cd: rca/bmg 74321 212922

romeo and juliet, excerpts from the ballet

boston 13 february 1967	boston so	lp: victor LM 2994/LSC 2994/LSC 3061/ SB 6749/GL 42699
los angeles 18-20 july 1977	los angeles philharmonic	lp: sheffield lab SLS 10043 cd: sheffield lab LAB 8

scythian suite

boston 24 october 1966	boston so	lp: victor LM 2934/LSC 2934/ RB 6705/SB 6705

GIACOMO PUCCINI (1858-1924)

la boheme

rome	rome opera	lp: victor LM 6095/LSC 6095/
15-30	orchestra	RE 5500-5501/SER 5500-5501/
june	and chorus	VL 43541
1961	moffo	cd: rca/bmg GD 83969/09026 601892
	costa	*excerpts*
	tucker	lp: victor LM 2655/LSC 2655/LSC 9914/
	merrill	RB 6562/SB 6562
	tozzi	cd: rca/bmg GD 60189
		excerpts also issued on lp by readers digest

la boheme, excerpt (si mi chiamano mimi)

new york	columbia so	78: columbia (usa) 71320D
18 august	sayao	78: columbia (argentina) 264742
1941		cd: sony MHK 63221

la fanciulla del west, excerpt (ch' ella mi creda libero)

new york	rca victor	78: victor 10-1482
17 march	orchestra	45: victor WDM 1250
1949	peerce	lp: victor VIC 1672/VICS 1672

puccini **madama butterfly**

rome
1-18
july
1957
	rome opera
	orchestra
	and chorus
	moffo
	elias
	valletti
	cesari
		lp: victor LM 6135/LSC 6135/LMDS 6135/
		    VIC 6100/VICS 6100/VL 43542
		cd: rca/bmg GD 84145
		excerpts
		lp: victor LM 9947/LSC 9947
		cd: rca/bmg RD 41452/GD 60202/
		    09026 601892/74321 394972
		excerpts also issued on lp by readers digest

new york 27 december 1958	metropolitan opera orchestra and chorus albanese miller morell guarrera	unpublished met broadcast

rome
10-20
july
1962
	rca italiana
	orchestra
	and chorus
	price
	elias
	tucker
	maero
		lp: victor LM 6160/LSC 6160/LMDS 6160/
		    RE 5504-5506/SER 5504-5506
		cd: rca/bmg RD 86160/74321 394972/
		    09026 688842
		excerpts
		lp: victor LM 2840/LSC 2840/RB 6505/
		    RB 6542/RB 6680/SB 6505/
		    SB 6542/SB 6680
		cd: rca/bmg 09026 681532

madama butterfly, excerpt (un bel di)

new york 18 august 1941	columbia so sayao	78: columbia (usa) 71320D 78: columbia (argentina) 264742 cd: sony MHK 63221

196
puccini **il tabarro**

walthamstow	new	lp: victor LSC 3220/SER 5619
28 june-	philharmonia	cd: rca/bmg GD 60865/09026 608652
2 july	alldis choir	
1971	price	
	dominguez	
	domingo	
	milnes	

tosca

rome   rome opera   lp: victor LM 6052/LSC 6052/
2-18   orchestra   RB 16051-16052/VIC 6000/
july   and chorus   VICS 6000/VL 43535
1957   milanov   cd: rca/bmg GD 84514
              bjoerling   *excerpts*
              warren   45: victor ERA 9796
                              lp: victor LM 2570/LM 9811/
                                  LSC 2570/LSC 9811/VIC 1672/
                                  VIC 1740/VICS 1672/VICS 1740
                              cd: rca/bmg GD 60192/RD 85934
                              cd: metropolitan opera MET 107
                              complete opera also issued unofficially on
                              cd by historic performers; excerpts also
                              issued on lp by readers digest

puccini **tosca,** excerpt (recondita armonia)

new york	rca victor	78: victor 10-1486
17 march	orchestra	45: victor WDM 1250
1949	peerce	

turandot

rome	rome opera	lp: victor LM 6149/LSC 6149/VL 43537/
3-11	orchestra	RE 25020-25022/SER 4520-4522/
july	and chorus	SER 5643-5645
1959	nilsson	cd: rca/bmg RD 85932/09026 626872
	tebaldi	*excerpts*
	bjoerling	lp: victor LM 2539/LM 9875/
	tozzi	LSC 2539/LSC 9875/RB 16267/
		SB 2138
		cd: rca/bmg RD 85934/09026 684292/
		09026 637052

SERGEI RACHMANINOV (1873-1943)

piano concerto no 2

london 8 july 1946	london philharmonic lympany	78: decca K 1545-1549/AK 1545-1549 78: london (usa) EDA 32
los angeles 4-5 march 1960	los angeles philharmonic pennario	lp: capitol P 8549/SP 8549

rhapsody on a theme of paganini

los angeles 22 september 1957	los angeles philharmonic pennario	lp: capitol P 8441/SP 8441

symphonic dances

rochester 29 april 1952	rochester philharmonic	lp: columbia (usa) ML 4621 lp: philips ABR 4064

MAURICE RAVEL (1875-1937)

piano concerto in g

boston 16 february 1963	boston so hollander	lp: victor LM 2667/LSC 2667/ RB 6546/SB 6546

piano concerto for the left hand

london 13 september 1960	philharmonia browning	lp: capitol P 8545/SP 8545 lp: angel 60224 cd: emi CDM 565 9232

daphnis et chloé, second suite

los angeles 16-18 march 1957	los angeles philharmonic	lp: capitol P 8395/SP 8395 cd: emi CDM 565 4252

pavane pour une infante défunte

new york 1 may 1948	nbc so	v-disc 846 *includes spoken introduction by leinsdorf*
new york 1953	silvertone so	lp: silvertone (usa) 119 lp: mercury (usa) MG 10021

NIKOLAI RIMSKY-KORSAKOV (1844-1908)

symphony no 2 "antar"

cleveland 22 february 1946	cleveland orchestra	78: columbia (usa) M 834 lp: columbia (usa) ML 2044

scheherazade, symphonic suite

los angeles 8-10 march 1960	los angeles philharmonic baker	lp: capitol P 8538/SP 8538 cd: emi CDM 565 4242

le coq d'or, suite

boston 25 november 1963	boston so	victor unpublished
boston 23-24 april 1964	boston so	lp: victor LM 2725/LSC 2725/ RB 6617/SB 6617/GL 42700

russian easter festival overture

los angeles 3-7 march 1958	concert arts orchestra	lp: capitol P 8446/SP 8446 cd: emi CDM 565 2052

GIOACHINO ROSSINI (1792-1868)

il barbiere di siviglia

new york	metropolitan	lp: victor 6143/LSC 6143/
1-12	opera orchestra	RE 25013-25015/SER 4511-4513/
september	and chorus	VIC 6102/VICS 6102/VL 43543
1958	peters	cd: rca/bmg GD 86505/09026 685522
	valletti	*excerpts*
	merrill	lp: victor LM 6071/LM 6171/LSC 6071/
	corena	LSC 6171/RB 6542/SB 6542
	tozzi	cd: rca/bmg 09026 601882
		excerpts also issued on lp by readers digest

il barbiere di siviglia, excerpt (la calumnia e un venticello)

new york	rca victor	78: victor
6 november	orchestra	cd: rca/bmg 09026 612452
1951	pinza	

il barbiere di siviglia, excerpt (a un dottor della mia sorte)

new york	columbia so	78: columbia (usa) 71193D
6 february	baccaloni	78: columbia (canada) 15502
1941		78: columbia (australia) LOX 522
		78: columbia (argentina) 266020

rossini **l'italiana in algeri, overture**

london philharmonia lp: capitol P 8465/SP 8465
20 may
1958

guilleaume tell, ballet music

los angeles concert arts lp: capitol P 8488/SP 8488
8 march orchestra
1958

CARL RUGGLES (1876-1971)

angels

chicago chicago so cd: chicago symphony orchestra
15-17 CSO 9010
december
1983

CAMILLE SAINT-SAENS (1835-1921)

introduction and rondo capriccioso for violin and orchestra
brent	new	lp: victor ARL1-0781
14-16	philharmonia	
august	fodor	
1974		

samson et dalila, bacchanale
los angeles	concert arts	lp: capitol P 8488/SP 8488
8 march	orchestra	cd: emi CDM 565 2052
1958		

FRANZ XAVER SCHARWENKA (1850-1924)

piano concerto no 1
boston	boston so	lp: victor LSC 3080
20 january	wild	cd: elan ELAN 82266
1969		

ARNOLD SCHOENBERG (1874-1951)

gurrelieder, introduction and song of the wood dove
boston	boston so	lp: victor LM 2785/LSC 2785/
19 october	chookasian	RB 6609/SB 6609
1964		

a survivor from warsaw
boston	boston so	lp: victor LSC 7055
23 april	new england	cd: rca/bmg 09026 636822
1969	chorus	
	milnes	

FRANZ SCHUBERT (1797-1828)

symphony no 8 "unfinished"

rochester   rochester   lp: columbia (usa) RL 3070/HL 7054/
3 april   philharmonic   OK 5018
1953

mass in e flat d950

berlin   berlin   lp: capitol P 8579/SP 8579
3-4   philharmonic   lp: electrola K 80725/STK 80725
september   st hedwig's   lp: emi 1C053 80005
1960   choir   lp: angel 60243
                   lorengar   cd: emi CZS 572 9542
                   allen   cd: testament SBT 1111
                   wunderlich
                   greindl

schubert **rosamunde, overture**

rochester
24 march
1954	rochester
philharmonic	lp: columbia (usa) RL 3102/HL 7105

rosamunde, entr'acte in b minor (ballet music no 1)

rochester
2 april
1954	rochester
philharmonic	45: philips CFE 15057/C496 038E
lp: columbia (usa) RL 3102/HL 7105

rosamunde, ballet music no 2

cleveland
25 february
1946	cleveland
orchestra	78: columbia (usa) 12749D
rochester
2 april
1954	rochester
philharmonic	45: philips CFE 15057/C496 038E
lp: columbia (usa) RL 3102/HL 7105

GUNTHER SCHULLER (born 1925)

seven studies on themes of paul klee
boston 23 november 1964	boston so	lp: victor LM 2879/LSC 2879/ RB 6677/SB 6677

ROBERT SCHUMANN (1810-1856)

symphony no 1 "spring"
cleveland 24-25 february 1946	cleveland orchestra	78: columbia (usa) M 617 lp: columbia (usa) ML 4794 lp: philips A01605

symphony no 4
boston 5-6 january 1963	boston so	lp: victor LM 2701/LSC 2701/ RB 6582/SB 6582 cd: rca/bmg VD 60488/09026 604882/ 09026 618552/74321 212842
london undated	philharmonia	unpublished radio broadcast

DIMITRI SHOSTAKOVICH (1906-1975)

symphony no 1
boston 26 september 1964	boston so	cd: boston symphony orchestra centennial edition

JEAN SIBELIUS (1865-1957)

symphony no 5
london	london	78: decca AK 2193-2196
9-13	philharmonic	78: london (usa) LA 142
july		
1946		

violin concerto
boston	boston so	lp: victor LM 2962/LSC 2962/
21 december	perlman	RB 6722/SB 6722
1966		cd: rca/bmg GD 86520/07863 565202/
		09026 635912

alla marcia/karelia suite
london	london	78: decca AK 2196
9-13	philharmonic	78: london (usa) LA 142
july		
1946		

BEDRICH SMETANA (1824-1884)

the moldau/ma vlast
los angeles	concert arts	lp: capitol P 8446/SP 8446
3-7	orchestra	cd: emi CDM 565 2052
march		
1958		
boston	boston so	cd: boston symphony orchestra
22 april		centennial edition
1967		

JOHN PHILIP SOUSA (1854-1932)

stars and stripes forever, march
boston	boston so	lp: victor LM 2757/LSC 2757
8 april		
1964		

EDUARD STRAUSS (1835-1916)

bahn frei, polka

cleveland 25 february 1946 | cleveland orchestra | 78: columbia (usa) 12543D

JOHANN STRAUSS I (1804-1849)

radetzky march

cleveland 25 february 1946 | cleveland orchestra | 78: columbia (usa) 12543D

JOHANN STRAUSS II (1825-1899)

perpetuum mobile

cleveland 25 february 1946	cleveland orchestra	78: columbia (usa) 12543D

unter donner und blitz, polka

cleveland 25 february 1946	cleveland orchestra	78: columbia (usa) 12543D
new york 24 april 1948	nbc so	us forces v-disc 846

JOSEF STRAUSS (1827-1870)

jockey polka

new york 24 april 1948	nbc so	us forces v-disc 846

sphärenklänge, waltz

cleveland 25 february 1946	cleveland orchestra	78: columbia (usa) 12579D

RICHARD STRAUSS (1864-1949)

die ägyptische helena, excerpt (zweite brautnacht)

boston 22-24 april 1965	boston so price	lp: victor LM 2849/LSC 2849/ RB 6639/SB 6639 cd: rca/bmg GD 60398/09026 681532

arabella

new york 9 february 1957	metropolitan opera orchestra and chorus della casa güden hurley lipton crain london alvary	unpublished met broadcast
new york 21 january 1961	metropolitan opera orchestra and chorus della casa rothenberger hurley dunn morell london herbert	unpublished met broadcast

strauss **ariadne auf naxos**
vienna	vienna	lp: victor LM 6152/LSC 6152/LMDS 6152/
2-10	philharmonic	RE 25023-25025/SER 4523-4525
june	rysanek	lp: decca 2BB 112-114
1959	peters	lp: london (usa) OSA 13100
	jurinac	cd: decca 443 6752
	peerce	*excerpts*
	berry	lp: decca 414 1771

divertimento after couperin
1987	chamber orchestra of europe	cd: asv records COE 809

don juan
garmisch	berlin	unpublished video recording
june	staatskapelle	
1991		

feuersnot
berlin	berlin radio	unpublished radio broadcast
may	orchestra	
1978	rias and tölz	
	choirs	
	janowitz	
	krebs	
	berger-tuna	
	shirley-quirk	

die frau ohne schatten, interludes arranged by leinsdorf
london	philharmonia	lp: capitol P 8548/SP 8548
12-16		cd: emi CDM 565 6132
september		
1960		

die frau ohne schatten, excerpt (sieh amme, sieh des mannes aug')
walthamstow	new	lp: victor ARL1-0333/TRL1-7044
9-11	philharmonia	cd: rca/bmg GD 60398/GD 86722/
july	ambrosian	09026 681532
1973	singers	
	price	
	clark	

strauss **le bourgeois gentilhomme, incidental music**

1987	chamber orchestra of europe	cd: asv records COE 809

guntram, excerpt (fass' ich sie bang)

walthamstow 9-11 july 1973	new philharmonia price	lp: victor ARL1-0333 cd: rca/bmg GD 60398

ein heldenleben

boston 9-10 march 1963	boston so	lp: victor LM 2641/LSC 2641/ RB 6565/SB 6565 cd: rca/bmg 74321 292502
garmisch june 1991	berlin staatskapelle	unpublished video recording

three hölderlin hymns (an die liebe; rückkehr in die heimat; die liebe)

garmisch june 1991	berlin staatskapelle hass	unpublished video recording

strauss **der rosenkavalier**

new york 26 december 1959	metropolitan opera orchestra and chorus della casa söderström ludwig fernandi czerwenka herbert	unpublished met broadcast

der rosenkavalier, excerpt (da geht er hin)

walthamstow 9-11 july 1973	new philharmonia price	lp: victor ARL1-0333/TRL1-7044 cd: rca/bmg GD 60398

der rosenkavalier, suite arranged by leinsdorf

london 17 september 1960	philharmonia	capitol unpublished
london 10-12 february 1969	london so	lp: decca PFS 4187 lp: london (usa) SPC 21037

salome

walthamstow 21-30 june 1968	london so caballé resnik lewis milnes	lp: victor LSC 7053/LMDS 7053/ SER 5582-5583 cd: rca/bmg GD 86644

strauss **salome, excerpt** (du wolltest mich deinen mund nicht küssen lassen)

boston 22-24 april 1965	boston so price	lp: victor LM 2849/LSC 2849/ 　　　RB 6639/SB 6639 cd: rca/bmg GD 60398/09026 681532

salome, dance of the seven veils

london 15-16 september 1960	philharmonia	lp: capitol P 8548/SP 8548
boston 22-24 april 1965	boston so	lp: victor LM 2849/LSC 2849/ 　　　RB 6639/SB 6639 cd: rca/bmg 09026 603982

strauss **till eulenspiegels lustige streiche**

london 12-16 september 1960	philharmonia	lp: capitol P 8548/SP 8548 cd: emi CDM 565 6132
london undated	philharmonia	unpublished radio broadcast

tod und verklärung

los angeles 13 july 1961	los angeles philharmonic	lp: capitol P 8580/SP 8580 cd: emi CDM 565 4252

vier letzte lieder

walthamstow 6-7 july 1973	new philharmonia price	lp: victor ARL1-0333 cd: rca/bmg GD 86722/09026 681532/ 74321 178962 *beim schlafengehen* cd: rca/bmg 09026 681522

IGOR STRAVINSKY (1882-1971)

agon
boston	boston so	lp: victor LM 2879/LSC 2879/
19 april		RB 6677/SB 6677
1965		

l'oiseau de feu, suite
boston	boston so	lp: victor LM 2725/LSC 2725/RB 6617/
23-24		SB 6617/GL 42700
april		cd: rca/bmg VD 60541/09026 605412
1964		

culver city	los angeles	lp: sheffield lab SLS 10043
29 april	philharmonic	cd: sheffield lab LAB 24
1985		

stuttgart	sdr orchestra	cd: mediaphon JA 75.103
1989		

petrushka, 1911 version
london	new	lp: decca PFS 4207/VIV 42
15 june	philharmonia	lp: london (usa) SLC 5037
1970		

le sacre du printemps
london	london	lp: decca PFS 4307/VIV 31
15 december	philharmonic	lp: london (usa) SPC 21114/STS 15590
1973		

violin concerto
boston	boston so	lp: victor LM 2852/LSC 2852
22-23	silverstein	
april		
1965		

PIOTR TCHAIKOVSKY (1840-1893)

symphony no 6 "pathétique"
los angeles 6-7 march 1960	los angeles philharmonic	lp: capitol P 8530/SP 8530 lp: emi MFP 2007

piano concerto no 1
los angeles 4 september 1957	los angeles philharmonic pennario	lp: capitol P 8417/SP 8417
boston 5 march 1963	boston so rubinstein	lp: victor LM 2681/LSC 2681/LSC 3305/ RB 6551/SB 6551/VCS 7070/ DPS 2014/RL 43195/AGL1-5217/ CRL7-0725 cd: rca/bmg GD 61262/RD 86259/ 09026 612622/09026 684542/ 09026 630372/09026 630002
boston 12 december 1966	boston so dichter	lp: victor LM 2954/LSC 2954/ RB 6707/SB 6707

violin concerto
boston 18-19 december 1967	boston so perlman	lp: victor LSC 3014/SB 6768/VICS 2000 cd: rca/bmg GD 86526/09026 635912
brent 14-16 august 1974	new philharmonia fodor	lp: victor ARL1-0781

violin concerto, abridged version of third movement
new york 3-4 april 1950	rca victor orchestra mischakoff	78: victor M 1428 45: victor WDM 1428 lp: victor LM 1101 *recorded for an album entitled heart of the violin concerto*

tchaikovsky **marche slave**

boston   boston so   lp: victor LM 2757/LSC 2757
13 april
1964

theme and variations/suite no 3

london   london   78: decca AK 1987-1988
24 june   philharmonic
1946

casse noisette, ballet suite

rochester   rochester   lp: columbia (usa) HL 7057/OK 5005
20 march   philharmonic   lp: hollywood (usa) LPH 135
1955   *excerpts*
                                   45: philips EFF 508

romeo and juliet, fantasy overture

new york   silvertone   78: silvertone (usa) S 1-2
1947   symphony   lp: silvertone (usa) 119
                orchestra   lp: mercury (usa) MG 10021
                                   lp: hollywood (usa) LPH 135

GIUSEPPE VERDI (1813-1901)

aida

walthamstow
9-23
july
1970
	london so
	alldis choir
	price
	bumbry
	domingo
	milnes
	raimondi
		lp: victor LSC 6198/LMDS 6198/
		    SER 5609-5611
		cd: rca/bmg RD 86198/74321 394982
		excerpts
		lp: victor LSC 3275/OPO 1003/RL 42090
		lp: metropolitan opera MET 104
		cd: rca/bmg 09026 616342/09026 681532/
		    09026 670622
		excerpts also issued on lp by readers digest

aida, dance of the moorish slaves and ballet music

los angeles 8 march 1958	concert arts orchestra	lp: capitol P 8488/SP 8488 cd: emi CDM 565 2052

un ballo in maschera

rome
8-21
june
1966
	rca italiana
	orchestra
	and chorus
	price
	grist
	verrett
	bergonzi
	merrill
	flagello
		lp: victor LM 6179/LSC 6179/LMDS 6179/
		    RE 5556-5558/SER 5710-5712
		cd: rca/bmg GD 86645/
		excerpts
		lp: victor LM 3034/LSC 3034/
		    VCS 7063/DPS 2001
		lp: metropolitan opera MET 104
		cd: rca/bmg RCD 17016/09026 681532
		excerpts also issued on lp by readers digest

don carlo, excerpt (ella giammai m'amo)

new york 6 november 1951	rca victor orchestra pinza	78: victor lp: victor LM 1751

verdi **la forza del destino, overture**

london 27 may 1958	philharmonia	lp: capitol P 8465/SP 8465

macbeth

new york
12-16
february
1959
	metropolitan
	opera orchestra
	and chorus
	rysanek
	bergonzi
	warren
	hines
		lp: victor LM 6147/LSC 6147/LMDS 6147/
		    RE 25006-25008/SER 4505-4507/
		    VL 43543
		cd: rca/bmg GD 84516
		excerpts
		45: victor ERA 9793
		lp: victor LM 9860/LSC 9860
		cd: rca/bmg 74321 377192
		cd: leonard warren commemorative LWC 1-2
		recording completed on 1-4 march 1959

new york 21 february 1959	metropolitan opera orchestra and chorus rysanek bergonzi warren hines	lp: movimento musica 03.029 lp: melodram MEL 085 cd: arkadia CD 471/CDMP 471
new york 2 january 1960	metropolitan opera orchestra and chorus rysanek barioni warren hines	unpublished met broadcast

otello, excerpts (dio mi potevi; niun mi tema)

new york	columbia so	78: columbia (usa) 71389D
15 april	melchior	78: columbia (argentina) 264748
1942		45: philips SBF 288
		lp: columbia (usa) Y 31740

rigoletto, excerpts (questa o quella; la donna e mobile)

new york	rca victor	78: victor 10-1528
17 march	orchestra	45: victor 49-0920
1949	peerce	

la traviata, excerpt (sempre libera)

new york	columbia so	78: columbia (usa) 71451D
9 march	sayao	78: columbia (brazil) 30-5185
1942		lp: columbia (usa) AAL 3/ML 4056
		cd: sony MHK 63221

i vespri siciliani, excerpt (o tu palermo)

new york	rca victor	78: victor
6 november	orchestra	45: victor ERA 40
1951	pinza	lp: victor LM 1751/RB 16040

messa da requiem

boston	boston so	lp: victor LM 7040/LSC 7040/
5-6	pro musica	RE 5537-5538/SER 5537-5538
october	chorus	*recording completed on 5 april 1965*
1964	nilsson	
	chookasian	
	bergonzi	
	flagello	

RICHARD WAGNER (1813-1883)

der fliegende holländer, overture

| boston
30 october
1967 | boston so | lp: victor LSC 3011/SB 6776 |

götterdämmerung

| new york
27 january
1962 | metropolitan
opera orchestra
and chorus
nilsson
kuchta
dalis
hopf
mittelmann
herbert
frick | unpublished met broadcast |

götterdämmerung, siegfried's funeral march

| los angeles
1-3 november
1957 | los angeles
philharmonic | lp: capitol P 8411/SP 8411
cd: emi CDM 565 6132 |
| culver city
18-20 july
1977 | los angeles
philharmonic | lp: sheffield lab SLS 10043
cd: sheffield lab LAB 7-8 |

for further orchestral music from götterdämmerung see later entry under orchestral synthesis from der ring des nibelungen

wagner **lohengrin**

new york 27 january 1940	metropolitan opera orchestra and chorus rethberg thorborg melchior huehn list warren	lp: ed smith EJS 135 cd: gebhardt 0007 cd: walhall WHL 18 cd: arkadia GA 2020
new york 17 january 1942	metropolitan opera orchestra and chorus varnay thorborg melchior janssen cordon warren	unpublished met broadcast
new york 2 january 1943	metropolitan opera orchestra and chorus varnay thorborg melchior sved cordon harrell	lp: ed smith UORC 170 cd: myto MCD 92466 *excerpts* cd: myto MCD 91341

wagner lohengrin/concluded

new york 24 february 1945	metropolitan opera orchestra and chorus varnay thorborg melchior sved cordon harrell	unpublished met broadcast

boston
23-28
august
1965
	boston so
	pro musica
	chorus
	amara
	gorr
	konya
	dooley
	hines
	marsh
		lp: victor LM 6710/LSC 6710/LMDS 6710/
		    RE 5544-5548/SER 5544-5548/
		    PVL5-9046
		cd: rca/bmg 74321 501642
		excerpts
		lp: victor LSC 10112

lohengrin, act three prelude

los angeles 1-3 november 1957	los angeles philharmonic	lp: capitol P 8411/SP 8411 cd: emi CDM 565 6132

wagner **lohengrin, excerpt (einsam in trüben tagen)**
new york	columbia so	78: columbia (usa) 71399D
10 april	varnay	lp: columbia (usa) SL 19089
1942		

lohengrin, excerpt (euch lüften die mein klagen)
new york	columbia so	78: columbia (usa) 71354D
10 april	varnay	lp: columbia (usa) SL 19089
1942		

lohengrin, excerpt (nun sei bedankt/mein held mein ritter!)
new york	columbia so	lp: columbia (usa) Y 31740
10 april	and chorus	lp: cbs 60200
1942	varnay	cd: sony MH2K 60896
	melchior	*unpublished columbia 78rpm recording*
	janssen	
	alvary	

die meistersinger von nürnberg
new york	metropolitan	lp: ed smith EJS 224
2 december	opera orchestra	lp: discocorp IGI 484
1939	and chorus	cd: walhall WHL 37
	jessner	
	branzell	
	kullmann	
	laufkötter	
	schorr	
	list	
	olitzki	
	janssen	

bayreuth	bayreuth	lp: melodram MEL 592
july	festival	
1959	orchestra	
	and chorus	
	grümmer	
	schärtel	
	schock	
	stolze	
	wiener	
	greindl	
	blankenheim	

wagner **die meistersinger von nürnberg, overture**

london 27 may 1958	philharmonia	lp: capitol P 8465/SP 8465
boston 30 october 1967	boston so	lp: victor LSC 3011/SB 6776

die meistersinger von nürnberg, dance of the apprentices and procession of the masters

los angeles 1-3 november 1957	los angeles philharmonic	lp: capitol P 8411/SP 8411

parsifal

new york 9 april 1960	metropolitan opera orchestra and chorus harshaw liebl uhde pechner hines wildermann	unpublished met broadcast

parsifal, act two

new york 15 april 1938	metropolitan opera orchestra flagstad melchior gabor	lp: ed smith EJS 484 *leinsdorf conducted only this act (and possibly conclusion of act one) of a complete performance due to the indisposition of artur bodansky*

wagner das rheingold

new york metropolitan unpublished met broadcast
16 december opera orchestra
1961 krall
 dalis
 madeira
 liebl
 kuen
 london
 herbert

rienzi, excerpt (all'mächtiger vater!)

new york columbia so 78: columbia (usa) 71388D
14 april melchior 78: columbia (canada) 15648
1942   78: columbia (australia) LOX 576
   78: columbia (argentina) 264747
   lp: columbia (usa) Y 31740
   lp: cbs 60200
   cd: sony MH2K 60896

siegfried

new york metropolitan unpublished met broadcast
13 january opera orchestra
1962 nilsson
 arroyo
 madeira
 hopf
 kuen
 london
 herbert
 frick

228
wagner **siegfried, excerpt (heil dir sonne!....to end of act three)**

rochester 9 april 1949	rochester philharmonic farrell svanholm	45: victor WDM 1319 lp: victor LM 1000/LM 2761/AVM1-1413

siegfried, forest murmurs

culver city 18-20 july 1977	los angeles philharmonic	lp: sheffield lab SLS 10043 cd: sheffield lab LAB 7-8

siegfried idyll

boston 1-2 october 1965	boston so	cd: boston symphony orchestra centennial edition

for further orchestral music from siegfried see later entry under orchestral synthesis from der ring des nibelungen

wagner **tannhäuser**

new york 25 march 1939	metropolitan opera orchestra and chorus flagstad thorborg farell melchior janssen list	unpublished met broadcast
new york 16 december 1939	metropolitan opera orchestra and chorus flagstad pauly stellman laholm janssen list	unpublished met broadcast *excerpts* lp: ed smith EJS 258
new york 4 january 1941	metropolitan opera orchestra and chorus flagstad thorborg stellman melchior janssen list	lp: ed smith GAW 300 lp: metropolitan opera guild MET 12 cd: arkadia CD 611/CDHP 611/GA 2032 cd: walhall WHL 7 cd: gebhardt JGCD 0006
new york 14 february 1942	metropolitan opera orchestra and chorus varnay thorborg stellman melchior janssen kipnis	unpublished met broadcast

wagner **tannhäuser, overture**

boston 19-22 december 1967	boston so	lp: victor LSC 3011/SB 6776

tannhäuser, overture and venusberg music

los angeles 8 march 1958	concert arts orchestra	lp: capitol P 8488/SP 8488 *overture only* cd: emi CDM 565 6132 *venusberg music only* cd: emi CDM 565 2082 *CDM 565 6132 states that recording made on 1-3 november 1957*
london 10-12 february 1969	london so	lp: decca PFS 4187 lp: london (usa) SPC 21037

tannhäuser, entry of the guests

boston 8 april 1964	boston so harvard and radcliffe choirs	lp: victor LM 2757/LSC 2757/LSC 5007

tannhäuser, excerpt (allmächt'ge jungfrau!)

new york 10 april 1942	columbia so varnay	78: columbia (usa) 71399D lp: columbia (usa) SL 19089

wagner **tristan und isolde**

new york 23 march 1940	metropolitan opera orchestra and chorus flagstad thorborg melchior huehn list cehanovsky	lp: ed smith UORC 182 cd: music and arts CD 647 *excerpts* lp: ed smith UORC 159 *UORC 182 incorrectly dated 1941; brief extracts from this 1940 performance also used to fill in gaps in the 1941 version listed below*
new york 8 february 1941	metropolitan opera orchestra and chorus flagstad thorborg melchior huehn kipnis darcy	lp: metropolitan opera guild MET 3 lp: melodram MEL 301 cd: metropolitan opera guild MET 3 cd: melodram CDM 37518 cd: gebhardt JGCD 0008 *excerpts* lp: acanta 40.23502 cd: simax PSC 1822 *sections missing from the recording are replaced by splices from the 1940 version listed above*
new york 6 february 1943	metropolitan opera orchestra and chorus traubel thorborg melchior huehn kipnis darcy	cd: arkadia GA 2010 cd: naxos 811.0010-0012 *excerpts* lp: ed smith EJS 556
new york 23 december 1944	metropolitan opera orchestra and chorus traubel thorborg melchior janssen kipnis darcy	unpublished met broadcast

wagner tristan und isolde/concluded
new york 30 january 1974	metropolitan opera orchestra and chorus nilsson vilma vickers plishka dooley lewis	lp: err records ERR 141-144

tristan und isolde, prelude with concert ending arranged by leinsdorf

new york 1950	silvertone symphony orchestra	lp: mercury MG 20014 lp: classic (france) 6040
boston 19 december 1967	boston so	lp: victor LSC 3011/SB 6776
culver city 18-20 july 1977	los angeles philharmonic	lp: sheffield lab SLS 10043 cd: sheffield lab LAB 7-8

tristan und isolde, prelude and liebestod

los angeles 13 july	los angeles philharmonic	lp: capitol P 8580/SP 8580 lp: angel 60344 cd: emi CDM 565 2082

tristan und isolde, excerpt (o könig das kann ich dir nicht sagen)

new york 14 april 1942	columbia so melchior	78: columbia (usa) 71388D 78: columbia (canada) 15648 78: columbia (australia) LOX 571 78: columbia (argentina) 264747 cd: sony MH2K 60896

wagner **tristan und isolde, excerpt (die alte weise)**
new york	columbia so	78: columbia (usa) M 550
15 april	melchior	cd: sony MHK 60896
1942	janssen	*in both these issues the scene continues with a recording made in buenos aires in 1943 with the same singers but not conducted by leinsdorf*

die walküre
new york	metropolitan	lp: ed smith UORC 186
17 february	opera orchestra	cd: arkadia GA 2015
1940	flagstad	cd: walhall WHL 14
	lawrence	
	branzell	
	melchior	
	huehn	
	list	
boston	metropolitan	cd: walhall WHL 1
30 march	opera orchestra	*excerpts*
1940	lawrence	lp: ed smith EJS 178-179
	lehmann	*recording of act three is incomplete*
	thorborg	
	melchior	
	schorr	
	list	
new york	metropolitan	cd: myto MCD 91341/982.H012
6 december	opera orchestra	cd: naxos 811.0058-0060
1941	traubel	*excerpts*
	varnay	lp: ed smith EJS 451/EJS 543
	thorborg	
	melchior	
	schorr	
	kipnis	
new york	metropolitan	unpublished met broadcast
27 february	opera orchestra	*excerpts*
1943	traubel	lp: ed smith EJS 100/EJS 171/UORC 158
	bampton	
	branzell	
	melchior	
	huehn	
	list	

wagner die walküre/concluded

walthamstow 9-23 september 1961	london so nilsson brouwenstijn gorr vickers london ward	lp: victor LD 6706/LDS 6706 lp: decca 7BB 125-129 cd: decca 430 3912 *excerpts* lp: victor LM 2692/LSC 2692/ 　　 RB 6658/SB 6658 lp: decca SDD 430/GRV 24
new york 23 december 1961	metropolitan opera orchestra nilsson kuchta dalis vickers edelmann wiemann	unpublished met broadcast

die walküre, ride of the valkyries

culver city	los angeles	lp: sheffield lab SLS 10043
18-20	philharmonic	cd: sheffield lab LAB 7-8
july		
1977		

die walküre, ride of the valkyries and magic fire music arranged by leinsdorf

los angeles	concert arts	lp: capitol P 8411/SP 8411
1-3	orchestra	cd: emi CDM 565 6132
november		
1957		

die walküre, excerpt (du bist der lenz)

new york	columbia so	78: columbia (usa) 71354D
10 april	varnay	lp: columbia (usa) SL 19089/3216 0304
1942		

der ring des nibelungen, orchestral synthesis arranged by leinsdorf (ride of the valkyries; magic fire music; siegfried penetrates the fire surrounding brünnhild's rock; dawn and rhine journey; transformation music after hagen's watch; funeral march; immolation and coda)

baden-baden	südwestfunk	cd: orchestrola (germany) ORC 77301
1977	orchestra	*also unpublished video recording*

CARL MARIA VON WEBER (1786-1826)

der freischütz, overture

london 9-13 july 1946	london philharmonic	78: decca K 1589

oberon, overture

london 20 may 1958	philharmonia	lp: capitol P 8465/SP 8465

KURT WEILL (1900-1950)

kleine dreigroschenmusik

boston 25 april 1969	boston so	lp: victor LSC 3121/SB 6827
chicago 23-25 may 1985	chicago so	cd: chicago symphony orchestra CSO 9010

HENRI WIENIAWSKI (1835-1880)

violin concerto no 2, second movement

new york 3-4 april 1950	rca victor orchestra mischakoff	78: victor M 1428 45: victor WDM 1428 lp: victor LM 1101 *recorded for an album entitled heart of the violin concerto*

MISCELLANEOUS

erich leinsdorf interviewed in german by marcel prawy

garmisch june 1991	unpublished video recording *bayerischer rundfunk*

unspecified rehearsal extracts

boston undated	boston so	cd: boston symphony orchestra centennial edition awaiting publication

georg solti
1912-1997

caricature of georg solti by rolf peter bauer

JOHANN SEBASTIAN BACH (1685-1750)

brandeburg concerto no 1
chicago   chicago so   decca unpublished
26 january
1980

brandenburg concerto no 2
chicago   chicago so   decca unpublished
26 january
1980

air/orchestral suite no 3
chicago   chicago so   lp: chicago symphony orchestra
14-15   DPM 10444
may
1974

matthäus-passion
chicago   chicago so   lp: decca 421 1771
23-31   and chorus   cd: decca 421 1772
march   kanawa   *excerpts*
1987   otter   cd: decca 425 6912
                       blochwitz
                       rolfe-johnson
                       krause
                       bär

mass in b minor
chicago   chicago so   cd: decca 430 3532
25-28   and chorus
january   lott
1990   otter
                       blochwitz
                       shimell
                       howell

BELA BARTOK (1881-1945)

concerto for orchestra

cologne 9 may 1955	wdr orchestra	unpublished radio broadcast
london 15-26 february 1965	london so	lp: decca LXT 6212/SXL 6212/JB 144 lp: london (usa) CM 9469/CS 6469/ CS 6784/JL 41037 cd: decca 425 0392
chicago 19 january 1980	chicago so	lp: decca SXDL 7536 lp: london (usa) LDR 71036 cd: decca 400 0522/417 7542
munich 19 february 1981	bavarian radio orchestra	cd: bavarian radio orchestra 50 years *rehearsal extract only*
budapest november 1990	chicago so	vhs video: decca 071 1273
geneva 5 july 1995	world peace orchestra	cd: decca 448 9012 vhs video: decca 071 1183

music for percussion, strings and celesta

london 21-23 february 1955	london philharmonic	lp: decca LXT 5059/ECM 533/ECS 533 lp: london (usa) LL 709/LLP 1230/CM 9132 lp: turnabout TV 34613
london 10-14 december 1963	london so	lp: decca LXT 6111/SXL 6111 lp: london (usa) CM 9399/CS 6399/CS 6783
chicago 13 may 1989	chicago so	cd: decca 430 3522

bartok **dance suite**

london 11-12 november 1952	london philharmonic	lp: decca LXT 2771/ECM 533/ECS 533 lp: london (usa) LL 709
london 7 may 1965	london so	lp: decca LXT 6212/SXL 6212/JB 144 lp: london (usa) CM 9469/CS 6469/ CS 6784/JL 41037 cd: decca 425 0392
chicago 11 december 1965	chicago so	cd: chicago symphony orchestra CD 892892
chicago 19 january 1980	chicago so	lp: decca SXDL 7536 lp: london (usa) LDR 71036 cd: decca 400 0522
budapest november 1990	chicago so	vhs video: decca 071 1273

divertimento for strings

chicago 11-16 november 1989	chicago so	cd: decca 430 3522 *recording completed 22 january-3 february 1990*

hungarian sketches

chicago november 1993	chicago so	cd: decca 443 4442

the miraculous mandarin, suite

london 17-31 december 1963	london so	lp: decca LXT 6111/SXL 6111 lp: london (usa) CM 9399/CS 6399/CS 6783 cd: decca 430 3522
chicago 13 may 1989	chicago so	cd: decca 430 3522

bartok **rumanian dances**

chicago november 1993	chicago so	cd: decca 443 4442
vienna april 1995	vienna philharmonic	vhs video: decca 071 1843

piano concerto no 1

london 8-9 april 1981	london philharmonic ashkenazy	lp: decca 410 1081 cd: decca 425 5732/448 1252

piano concerto no 2

london 16-17 march 1979	london philharmonic ashkenazy	lp: decca SXL 6937 lp: london (usa) CS 7167 cd: decca 425 5732/448 1252 *recording completed on 10 february 1980*

bartok **piano concerto no 3**

salzburg	vienna	unpublished radio broadcast
16 august	philharmonic	
1964	a.fischer	

london	london	lp: decca SXL 6937/410 1081
10-11	philharmonic	lp: london (usa) CS 7167
february	ashkenazy	cd: decca 411 9692/425 5732/448 1252
1978		

budapest	chicago so	vhs video: decca 071 1273
november	schiff	
1990		

violin concerto no 1

chicago	chicago so	lp: decca 411 8041
18 october	chung	cd: decca 411 9692/425 0152
1983		

violin concerto no 2

viersen	wdr orchestra	unpublished radio broadcast
18 september	varga	
1950		

london	london	lp: decca SXL 6082/411 8041
11-13	philharmonic	lp: london (usa) CS 7023
february	chung	cd: decca 411 8042/425 0152
1976		

two portraits for violin and orchestra

chicago	chicago so	cd: chicago symphony orchestra CD 0009
24-26	magad	
september		
1987		

sonata for two pianos and percussion

snape	perahia	lp: cbs M 42625
september	solti	cd: sony MK 42625
1982	corkhill	
	glennie	

246
bartok **cantata profana**

budapest	budapest	cd: decca 458 9292
june	festival	*also unpublished video recording of rehearsal*
1997	orchestra	*extract*
	hungarian	
	radio choir	
	daroczy	
	agache	

bluebeard's castle

london	london	lp: decca SET 630
19-21	philharmonic	lp: london (usa) OSA 1174
march	sass	cd: decca 433 0822
1979	kovats	vhs video: decca 071 1473
	sztankey	laserdisc: decca 071 1471
		excerpts
		lp: london philharmonic LPJ 50
		071 1473/1471 uses the recording as soundtrack to a film version

LUDWIG VAN BEETHOVEN (1770-1827)

symphony no 1
chicago 13-15 may 1974	chicago so	lp: decca 11BB 188-196/SXL 6760 lp: london (usa) CSP 9/CS 6926 cd: decca 421 6732/425 5322/430 7922
chicago 13-16 november 1989	chicago so	cd: decca 430 3202/430 4002

symphony no 2
chicago 18 may 1974	chicago so	lp: decca 11BB 188-196/SXL 6761 lp: london (usa) CSP 9/CS 6927 cd: decca 425 5322/430 7922/460 8422
chicago 22 january- 3 february 1990	chicago so	cd: decca 430 3202/430 4002

symphony no 3 "eroica"
vienna 3-13 may 1959	vienna philharmonic	lp: decca LXT 5537/SXL 2165 lp: london (usa) CM 9032/CS 6145/ CS 6778/JL 41040
chicago 5-9 november 1972	chicago so	lp: decca 11BB 188-196/SXL 6829 lp: london (usa) CSP 9/CS 7049 cd: decca 421 6732/425 5322/430 7922 *recording completed on 18 may 1974*
chicago 6-13 may 1989	chicago so	cd: decca 430 0872/430 4002
salzburg 30 july 1989	vienna philharmonic	unpublished video recording *funeral march only performed at a concert to mark the death of herbert von karajan*

beethoven **symphony no 4**

london 14-15 november 1950	london philharmonic	lp: decca LXT 2564/ACL 95 lp: london (usa) LL 319/B 19033
cologne 3 november 1952	wdr orchestra	unpublished radio broadcast
chicago 13 may 1974	chicago so	lp: decca 11BB 188-196/SXL 6830/417 6021 lp: london (usa) CSP 9/CS 7050 cd: decca 421 6732/425 5322/ 430 7922/460 8422
chicago 21-22 september 1987	chicago so	cd: decca 421 5802/430 4002

symphony no 5

vienna 17-25 september 1958	vienna philharmonic	lp: decca LXT 5510/SXL 2124/VIV 24 lp: london (usa) CM 9011/CS 6092/JL 41016
chicago 5-6 november 1973	chicago so	lp: decca 11BB 188-196/SXL 6762/417 6021 lp: london (usa) CSP 9/CS 6930 cd: decca 421 6732/425 5322/430 7922
chicago 6-7 october 1986	chicago so	cd: decca 421 5802/430 4002
tokyo 15 april 1990	chicago so	vhs video: sony SHV 46398 laserdisc: sony SLV 46398
vienna 5-6 may 1990	vienna philharmonic	cd: decca 430 5052/448 9452

beethoven **symphony no 6 "pastoral"**

vienna 5-6 november 1974	chicago so	lp: decca 11BB 188-196/SXL 6763 lp: london (usa) CSP 9/CS 6931 cd: decca 417 7652/421 6732/ 425 5322/430 7922
chicago 9-16 may 1988	chicago so	cd: decca 421 7732/430 4002 *recording completed on 18 october 1988*

symphony no 7

vienna 14-17 october 1958	vienna philharmonic	lp: decca LXT 5508/SXL 2121 lp: london (usa) CM 9012/CS 6093/CS 6777
vienna 9-10 september 1974	chicago so	lp: decca 11BB 188-196/SXL 6764 lp: london (usa) CSP 9/CS 6932 cd: decca 425 5322/430 7922/458 6552
london 1987	london so	laserdisc: pioneer (usa) PA 90292/PLMCB 00191 dvd: arthaus 100 148
chicago 14-16 may 1988	chicago so	cd: decca 425 5252/430 4002
chicago october 1991	chicago so	unpublished video recording
vienna april 1995	vienna philharmonic	vhs video: decca 071 1843

symphony no 8

cologne 21 january 1951	wdr orchestra	unpublished radio broadcast
chicago 6-9 november 1973	chicago so	lp: decca 11BB 188-196/SXL 6760 lp: london (usa) CSP 9/CS 6926 cd: decca 417 7652/421 6732/425 5322/ 430 7922/458 6552
chicago 17-18 october 1988	chicago so	cd: decca 425 5252/430 4002

beethoven **symphony no 9 "choral"**

chicago	chicago so	lp: decca 11BB 188-196/6BB 121-122/
15-16	and chorus	417 4861
may	lorengar	lp: london (usa) CSP 9/CSP 8
1972	minton	cd: decca 421 6732/430 4382/
	burrows	430 6352/430 7922
	talvela	*final movement*
		cd: decca 411 9572/425 4982
		rehearsal extracts
		lp: chicago symphony orchestra CSO 1000

chicago	chicago so	lp: decca 417 8001
29 september-	and chorus	cd: decca 417 8002/425 5322/430 4002
7 october	norman	
1986	runkel	
	schunk	
	sotin	

london	chicago so	unpublished radio broadcast and
13 september	bbc chorus	unpublished video recording
1996	london voices	
	voigt	
	otter	
	botha	
	pape	

piano concerto no 1

chicago	chicago so	lp: decca SXLG 6594-6597/SXL 6651
22-23	ashkenazy	lp: london (usa) OSA 2404/CS 6853
may		cd: decca 425 5822/443 7232
1972		

london	london so	laserdiscd: pioneer (usa) PA 90292/
1987	perahia	PLMCB 00191
		dvd: arthaus 100 148

piano concerto no 2

chicago	chicago so	lp: decca SXLG 6594-6597/SXL 6652
22-23	ashkenazy	lp: london (usa) OSA 2404/CS 6854
may		cd: decca 417 7032/425 5822/443 7232
1972		

beethoven **piano concerto no 3**
chicago   chicago so   lp: decca SXLG 6594-6597/SXL 6653/417 6011
11 may   ashkenazy   lp: london (usa) OSA 2404/CS 6855
1971   cd: decca 417 7402/425 5822/443 7232

piano concerto no 4
chicago   chicago so   lp: decca SXLG 6594-6597/SXL 6654/417 6011
22-23   ashkenazy   lp: london (usa) OSA 2404/CS 6856
may   cd: decca 417 7402/425 5822/
1972   436 3802/443 7232

piano concerto no 5 "emperor"
cologne   wdr orchestra   unpublished radio broadcast
25 june   backhaus
1956

chicago   chicago so   lp: decca SXLG 6594-6597/
10-11   ashkenazy   SXL 6655/VIV 37/417 2841
may   lp: london (usa) OSA 2404/CS 6857/CSP 12
1971   cd: decca 417 7032/425 5822/
                                         436 3802/443 7232

violin concerto
london   london   lp: decca LXT 5068/ECM 813
22-25   philharmonic   lp: london (usa) LL 1257
april   elman
1955

coriolan, overture
stockholm   swedish radio   lp: bis BISLP 331-333
22 february   orchestra
1958

cologne   wdr orchestra   unpublished radio broadcast
2 june
1958

vienna   chicago so   lp: decca 11BB 188-196/SXL 6655/SXL 6764
10 september   lp: london (usa) CSP 9/CS 6857/
1974   CS 6932/JL 41058
                                     cd: decca 421 6732/430 7922

london   london so   laserdisc: pioneer (usa) PA 90292/PLMCB 00191
1987   perahia   dvd: arthaus 100 148

beethoven **egmont overture**

zürich 25 june 1947	tonhalle- orchester	78: decca K 1904 lp: london (usa) LL 49 *solti's first orchestral recording for decca*

chicago
18-23
may
1972
	chicago so	lp: decca 11BB 188-196/SXL 6761/
		    SXL 6684/SXL 6927
		lp: london (usa) CSP 9/CS 6800/
		    CS 6857/CS 6927/JL 41058
		cd: decca 421 6732/430 7922/460 9822

chicago 13-16 november 1989	chicago so	cd: decca 430 0872/430 4002
tokyo 15 april 1990	chicago so	vhs video: sony SHV 46398 laserdisc: sony SLV 46398

fidelio

chicago 21-24 may 1979	chicago so and chorus behrens ghazarian hofmann kuebler sotin adam howell	lp: decca D178 D3 lp: london (usa) LDR 1001/ cd: decca 410 2272/455 0662 *excerpts* lp: decca SXDL 7529/DIG 2 lp: london (usa) JL 41058 cd: decca 430 7112/448 2502

fidelio, excerpt (heil sei dem tag! .... to end of opera)

london 25 february 1990	covent garden orchestra and chorus jones goldberg hale	unpublished radio broadcast *music performance research centre*
geneva 5 july 1995	world peace orchestra london voices herlitzius andersen tschammer	cd: decca 448 9012 vhs video: decca 071 1833

beethoven **fidelio, excerpt (mir ist so wunderbar)**
london	covent garden	lp: decca SET 392-393
22-23	orchestra	lp: london (usa) OSA 1276
february	jones	
1968	robson	
	dobson	
	kelly	

leonore no 3 overture
chicago	chicago so	lp: decca 11BB 188-196/SXL 6654/
18 may		SXL 6684/SXL 6762
1972		lp: london (usa) CSP 9/CS 6800/
		CS 6856/CS 6930/JL 41058
		cd: decca 421 6732/430 7922/460 9822

chicago	chicago so	cd: decca 421 7732/430 4002
10-16		*recording completed on 11 october 1988*
may		
1988		

john holmes (conductors on record) also mentions a recording of the overture by solti and zürich tonhalle-orchester but this cannot be traced

missa solemnis
chicago	chicago so	lp: decca D87 D2/411 8421
16-18	and chorus	cd: london (usa) OSA 12111
may	popp	cd: decca 411 8422/425 8442/455 0142
1977	minton	
	walker	
	howell	

berlin	berlin	cd: decca 444 3372
15-16	philharmonic	
march	rundfunkchor	
1994	varady	
	vermillion	
	cole	
	pape	

violin sonata no 9 "kreutzer"
zürich	kulenkampff	78: decca K 28119-28122
july	solti, piano	lp: decca ACL 211/ECM 832
1948		lp: decca (germany) KD 11020
		lp: london (usa) CM 9507/R 23214
		cd: urania URN 22.112

ALBAN BERG (1885-1935)

violin concerto
chicago	chicago so	lp: decca 411 8041
17-18	chung	cd: decca 411 8042/452 6962/460 0052
october		
1983		

HECTOR BERLIOZ (1803-1869)
symphonie fantastique

chicago	chicago so	lp: decca SXL 6571/414 3071
17-18		lp: london (usa) CS 6790
may 1972		cd: decca 417 7052/430 4412

salzburg	chicago so	cd: decca 436 8392
8 june		
1992		

la damnation de faust

edinburgh	covent garden	unpublished radio broadcast
18 august	orchestra	*music performance research centre*
1963	and chorus	
	veasey	
	gedda	
	london	

chicago	chicago so	lp: decca D259 D3
4-7	and chorus	lp: london (usa) LDR 73007
may	stade	cd: decca 414 6802
1981	riegel	*excerpts*
	van dam	cd: decca 410 1812

london	chicago so	vhs video: decca 071 1093
july	and chorus	
1989	otter	
	lewis	
	van dam	

marche hongroise/la damnation de faust

tokyo	chicago so	vhs video: sony SHV 46398
15 april		laserdisc: sony SLV 46398
1990		

vienna	vienna	vhs video: decca 071 1843
april 1995	philharmonic	

les francs juges, overture

chicago	chicago so	lp: decca SXL 6684/414 3071
9 november		cd: decca 417 7052/430 4412/
1973		430 6352/460 9822
		recording completed on 18 may 1974; also
		private lp issue for chicago symphony orchestra

roméo et juliette, orchestral excerpts

chicago	chicago so	laserdisc: decca 071 1011
17-18		
october 1977		

GEORGES BIZET (1838-1875)
carmen

london 4 july 1973	covent garden orchestra and chorus verrett kanawa domingo van dam	unpublished radio broadcast *music performance research centre*
london 2-13 july 1975	london philharmonic alldis choir troyanos kanawa domingo van dam	lp: decca D11 D3 lp: london (usa) OSA 13115 cd: decca 414 4892 *excerpts* lp: decca SET 621/SET 622/GRV 22 cd: decca 417 6452/421 3002/421 8902/ 433 0642/433 0672/433 8222/ 436 2862/436 3002/436 3102/ 436 4652/436 6032/440 4102/ 440 9472/443 3782/443 5952/ 444 6152/448 0532/448 1352/ 458 2042/460 9822 *recording completed on 15 december 1975;* *sessions 10-13 july used national philharmonic* *orchestra conducted by sidney sax*

carmen, prelude

london 22-23 february 1968	covent garden orchestra	lp: decca SET 392-393/SPA 127 lp: london (usa) OSA 1276/CS 6730

BORIS BLACHER (1903-1975)
paganini variations

vienna 19-22 april 1995	vienna philharmonic	cd: decca 452 8532

requiem

vienna june 1959	vienna symphony singakademie zadek rehfuss	unpublished radio broadcast *world premiere performance*

LUIGI BOCCHERINI (1743-1805)

cello concerto in b flat
hamburg	ndr orchestra	lp: replica RPL 2471
3 november	tortelier	
1958		

ARRIGO BOITO (1842-1918)

mefistofele, excerpt (l'altra notte)
chicago	lyric opera	lp: decca LXT 5326
10 november	orchestra	lp: london (usa) LL 1626/A 5320/SR 33157
1956	tebaldi	cd: decca 448 1542

ALEXANDER BORODIN (1833-1887)

prince igor, overture
berlin	berlin	lp: decca SPA 257
2-5	philharmonic	lp: london (usa) CS 6944/JL 41051
june		cd: polygram (japan) POCL 2013
1959		

london	london so	lp: decca LXT 6263/SXL 6263/411 8381
31 january-		lp: london (usa) CM 9503/CM9785/
3 february		CS 6503/CS 6785
1966		cd: decca 417 6892/444 3892/
		450 0172/455 6322/460 9822

chicago	chicago so	vhs video: classic (usa) LP 101
29 april		
1982		

prince igor, polovtsian dances
london	london so	lp: decca LXT 6263/SXL 6263/SET 622/
31 january-	lso chorus	SPA 127/411 8381
3 february		lp: london (usa) CM 9503/CM 9730/CM 9785/
1966		CS 6503/CS 6730/CS 6785
		cd: decca 417 6892/444 3892/
		450 0172/455 6322/460 9772

JOHANNES BRAHMS (1833-1897)

symphony no 1

edinburgh september 1971	chicago so	unpublished video recording *recorded at a concert during the orchestra's first visit to europe*
chicago 9-10 january 1979	chicago so	lp: decca D151 D4/SXL 6924/417 2861 lp: london (usa) OSA 2406/CS 7198 cd: decca 414 4582/421 0742/ 430 7992/452 3292

symphony no 2

cologne 16 february 1968	wdr orchestra	unpublished radio broadcast
chicago 9-10 january 1979	chicago so	lp: decca D151 D4/SXL 6925 lp: london (usa) OSA 2406/CS 7199 cd: decca 414 4872/421 0742/ 430 7992/452 3292

symphony no 3

chicago 22-24 may 1978	chicago so	lp: decca D151 D4/SXL 6902 lp: london (usa) OSA 2406/CS 7200 cd: decca 414 4882/430 7992/452 3322

symphony no 4

chicago 23-24 may 1978	chicago so	lp: decca D151 D4/SXL 6890/417 6071 lp: london (usa) OSA 2406/CS 7201 cd: decca 414 5632/430 4402/ 430 7992/452 3322

brahms **piano concerto no 1**
cologne 9 may 1955	wdr orchestra badura-skoda	unpublished radio broadcast
vienna 20-23 april 1988	vienna philharmonic schiff	lp: decca 425 1101 cd: decca 425 1102

haydn variations
chicago 23 may 1977	chicago so	lp: decca D135 D2/SXL 7004 lp: london (usa) OSA 12114/CS 6984/JL 41062 cd: decca 414 6272/430 4402/ 430 6352/452 3292
new york 21 june 1994	orchestra of the solti orchestral project	cd: decca 444 4582

haydn variations, version for two pianos
snape september 1982	perahia and solti, pianos	lp: cbs M 42625 cd: sony MK 42625

academic festival overture
chicago 24 may 1978	chicago so	lp: decca D151 D4/SXL 6902/417 2861 lp: london (usa) OSA 2406/CS 7200/JL 41062 cd: decca 414 4882/430 7992/ 452 3292/460 9822

tragic overture
cologne 3 november 1952	wdr orchestra	unpublished radio broadcast
chicago 24 may 1979	chicago so	lp: decca D151 D4/SXL 6925 lp: london (usa) OSA 2406/CS 7199/JL 41062 cd: decca 414 4872/421 0742/ 430 7992/452 3292

brahms **ein deutsches requiem**

frankfurt november 1954	frankfurt opera orchestra and chorus wissmann adam	lp: capitol (germany) PBR 8300
chicago 15-16 may 1978	chicago so and chorus kanawa weikl	lp: decca D135 D2 lp: london (usa) OSA 12114 cd: decca 414 6272/425 0422/452 3442

variations on a theme of robert schumann for two pianos

vienna 20-23 april 1988	schiff and solti, pianos	lp: decca 425 1101 cd: decca 425 1102

brahms **violin sonata no 1**

zürich	kulenkampff	78: decca K 23013-23015/AK 1705-1707
28 january	solti, piano	lp: decca ACL 250/ECM 832
1947		lp: london (usa) CM 9506/R 23213
		lp: decca (germany) KD 11010
		cd: urania URN 22.112

violin sonata no 2

zürich	kulenkampff	78: decca K 2083-2085
28 january	solti, piano	78: london (usa) T 5304-5306
1947		lp: decca ACL 250/ECM 832
		lp: london (usa) CM 9506/R 23213
		lp: decca (germany) KD 11010
		cd: urania URN 22.112

violin sonata no 3

zürich	kulenkampff	78: decca K 2112-2114
july	solti, piano	lp: decca ACL 250/ECM 832
1948		lp: decca (germany) KD 11020
		lp: london (usa) CM 9506/R 23213
		cd: urania URN 22.112

BENJAMIN BRITTEN (1913-1976)

billy budd, excerpt (o beauty, o handsomeness!)

| london 22-23 february 1968 | covent garden orchestra robinson | lp: decca SET 392-393
lp: london (usa) OSA 1276 |

a midsummer night's dream, excerpt (helena! hermia!)

| london 22-23 february 1968 | covent garden orchestra robson howells macdonald bryn-jones | lp: decca SET 392-393
lp: london (usa) OSA 1276 |

peter grimes, excerpt (embroidery in childhood)

| london 16-21 december 1996 | london so fleming summers | cd: decca 455 7602 |

young person's guide to the orchestra

| chicago 29 october 1979 | chicago so | decca unpublished |

ANTON BRUCKNER (1824-1896)

symphony no "0"

chicago   chicago so   cd: decca 448 9102/452 1602
5-7
october
1995

symphony no 1

chicago   chicago so   cd: decca 448 8982/448 9102
14-18
february
1995

symphony no 2

chicago   chicago so   cd: decca 436 8442/448 9102
12-14
october
1991

symphony no 3

chicago   chicago so   cd: decca 440 3162/448 9102
16-17
october
1992

munich   bavarian   unpublished video recording
10-11   radio
june   orchestra
1993

symphony no 4 "romantic"

chicago   chicago so   lp: decca SXDL 7538
26-27   lp: london (usa) LDR 71038
january   cd: decca 410 5502/448 9102
1981

bruckner **symphony no 5**

chicago 28-30 january 1980	chicago so	lp: decca D221 D2 lp: london (usa) LDR 10031 cd: decca 425 0082/448 9102

symphony no 6

chicago 10-12 january 1979	chicago so	lp: decca SXL 6946 lp: london (usa) CS 7173 cd: decca 417 3892/448 9102 *recording completed on 2 june 1979*
chicago 23-24 october 1979	chicago so	unpublished video recording

bruckner **symphony no 7**

vienna 20-28 october 1965	vienna philharmonic	lp: decca MET 323-324/SET 323-324 lp: london (usa) OSA 2216
london 5 september 1978	chicago so	vhs video: decca 071 1053 laserdisc: decca 071 1051
chicago 11 october 1986	chicago so	cd: decca 417 6312/448 9102

symphony no 8

vienna 28-29 november 1966	vienna philharmonic	lp: decca MET 335-336/SET 335-336 lp: london (usa) CMA 7219/CSA 1242 cd: decca 448 1242
leningrad 20-21 november 1990	chicago so	cd: decca 430 2882/448 9102

symphony no 9

chicago 30 september- 1 october 1985	chicago so	lp: decca 417 2951 cd: decca 417 2952/448 9102

ELLIOTT CARTER (born 1908)

variations for orchestra

los angeles   chicago so   cd: chicago symphony orchestra CD 0009
26 january
1982

JOHN CORIGLIANO (born 1938)

tournaments, overture

chicago   chicago so   cd: chicago symphony orchestra CD 9010
4-6
october
1984

PAUL CRESTON (1906-1985)

fantasy for trombone and orchestra

chicago   chicago so   unpublished radio broadcast
27 may   friedman
1976

CLAUDE DEBUSSY (1862-1918)
la mer
chicago	chicago so	lp: decca SXL 6813/417 6051
24 may		lp: london (usa) CS 7033
1976		cd: decca 430 4442/430 6352

chicago	chicago so	cd: decca 436 4682
10-12 december		
1991		

trois nocturnes
cologne	wdr orchestra	unpublished radio broadcast
2 june	and chorus	
1958		

chicago	chicago so	cd: decca 436 4682
10-12	and chorus	
december		
1991		

prélude a l'apres-midi d'un faune
chicago	chicago so	lp: decca SXL 6813/417 6051
24 may		lp: london (usa) CS 7033
1976		cd: decca 417 7042/430 4442/430 6352

chicago	chicago so	cd: decca 436 4682
10-12 december		
1991		

LEO DELIBES (1836-1891)
prélude and mazurka/coppélia
london	covent garden	unpublished radio broadcast
undated	orchestra	

DAVID DEL TREDICI (born 1937)
final alice
chicago	chicago so	lp: decca SXDL 7516
27-30	hendricks	lp: london (usa) LDR 71018
january		
1980		

ERNO DOHNANYI (1877-1960)
variations on a nursery song
chicago	chicago so	lp: decca 417 2941
8 october	schiff	cd: decca 417 2942
1985		

PAUL DUKAS (1865-1935)

l'apprenti sorcier

tel aviv	israel	45: decca CEP 547/SEC 5015
28-29	philharmonic	lp: decca LXT 5477/SXL 2007/ADD 109/
march		SDD 109/ECM 703/ECS 703
1957		lp: london (usa) LL 1715/CM 9202/CS 6005/
		STS 15005

ANTONIN DVORAK (1841-1904)

symphony no 9 "from the new world"

chicago	chicago so	lp: decca 411 1161
17-18		cd: decca 411 1162
january		
1983		

rusalka, excerpt (o silver moon!)

london	london so	cd: decca 455 7602
16-21	fleming	
december		
1996		

EDWARD ELGAR (1857-1934)

symphony no 1

london 21-25 february 1972	london philharmonic	lp: decca SXL 6569 lp: london (usa) CS 6789 cd: decca 421 3872/440 3222/443 8562

symphony no 2

london 14-15 february 1975	london philharmonic	lp: decca SXL 6723 lp: london (usa) CS 6941 cd: decca 421 3862/436 1502/443 8562

violin concerto

london 14-15 february 1977	london philharmonic chung	lp: decca SXL 6842 lp: london (usa) CS 7064 cd: decca 421 3892/440 3192/ 452 6962/460 0152

enigma variations

london 15 may 1974	london philharmonic	lp: decca SXL 6795/417 4561 lp: london (usa) CS 6984 cd: decca 417 7912/425 1552
vienna 19-22 june 1996	vienna philharmonic	cd: decca 452 8532

elgar **falstaff**

london	london	lp: decca SXL 6963
4-6	philharmonic	lp: london (usa) CS 7193
december		cd: decca 425 1552/ 440 3262
1979		

cockaigne, overture

london	london	lp: decca SXL 6795/SXL 6848
27 february	philharmonic	lp: london (usa) CS 7072
1976		cd: decca 417 7192/421 3872/440 3172/
		443 8562/443 9362

in the south, overture

london	london	lp: decca SXL 6963
4-6	philharmonic	lp: london (usa) CS 7193
december		cd: decca 421 3862/436 1502/
1979		440 3172/443 8562

pomp and circumstance, march no 1

london	london	lp: decca SXL 6848/417 4561
7-18	philharmonic	lp: london (usa) CS 7072
february		cd: decca 411 9542/417 7192/425 0862/
1979		425 8472/430 4472/430 6352/
		433 8702/436 9282/440 3172/
		443 5942/443 9362/461 2862

recording completed in march and april 1979

elgar pomp and circumstance, march no 2

london	london	lp: decca SXL 6848/417 4561
7-18	philharmonic	lp: london (usa) CS 7072
february		cd: decca 417 7192/440 3172
1979		*recording completed in march and april 1979*

pomp and circumstance, march no 3

london	london	lp: decca SXL 6848/417 4561
7-18	philharmonic	lp: london (usa) CS 7072
february		cd: decca 417 7192/440 3172
1979		*recording completed in march and april 1979*

pomp and circumstance, march no 4

london	london	45: decca F 13713
7-18	philharmonic	lp: decca SXL 6848/417 4561
february		lp: london (usa) CS 7072
1979		cd: decca 411 9542/417 7192/425 0862/ 430 4472/430 6352/440 3172/ 443 9362
		recording completed in march and april 1979

pomp and circumstance, march no 5

london	london	lp: decca SXL 6848/417 4561
7-18	philharmonic	lp: london (usa) CS 7072
february		cd: decca 417 7192/430 4472/ 430 6352/440 3172
1979		*recording completed in march and april 1979*

UMBERTO GIORDANO (1867-1948)

andrea chenier, excerpt (nemico della patria)

chicago	lyric opera	lp: decca LXT 5326
10 november	orchestra	lp: london (usa) LL 1626/A 5320
1956	bastianini	cd: decca 448 1542

MIKHAIL GLINKA (1804-1857)

russlan and lyudmila, overture

berlin	berlin	lp: decca SPA 257
2-5	philharmonic	lp: london (usa) CS 6944
june		cd: polygram (japan) POCL 2013
1959		
london	london so	lp: decca LXT 6263/SXL 6263/ SPA 127/411 8381
31 january-		
3 february		lp: london (usa) CM 9503/CM 9785/ CS 6503/CS 6730/CS 6785
1966		
		cd: decca 417 6892/450 0172/ 460 9772/460 9822
chicago	chicago so	cd: chicago symphony orchestra CSO 892892
27 may		
1976		

CHRISTOPH WILLIBALD GLUCK (1714-1787)

orfeo ed euridice
cologne	wdr orchestra	unpublished radio broadcast
march	and chorus	
1952	cavelti	
	della casa	
	lipp	
	sung in german	

london	covent garden	lp: decca SET 443-444
29 june-	orchestra	lp: london (usa) OSA 1285
9 july	and chorus	cd: decca 417 4102
1969	horne	*excerpts*
	lorengar	lp: london (usa) CS 6730/OS 26214
	donath	cd: decca 452 7352

CHARLES GOUNOD (1818-1893)

faust, ballet music
london	covent garden	45: decca CEP 668/SEC 5067
28 january	orchestra	lp: decca LXT 5642/SXL 2280/JB 12
1960		lp: london (usa) CM 9285/CS 6216/ CS 6780/JL 41029
		cd: decca 433 6212/448 9422

also undated and unpublished radio broadcast of unspecified movements from faust ballet music with covent garden orchestra

GEORGE FRIDERIC HANDEL (1685-1759)

messiah
chicago	chicago so	lp: decca 414 3961
1-9	and chorus	cd: decca 414 3962
october	kanawa	*excerpts*
1984	gjevang	cd: decca 417 4492/430 0982/ 430 7342/466 2152
	lewis	
	howell	

KARL AMADEUS HARTMANN (1905-1963)

symphony no 7
vienna	vienna	unpublished radio broadcast
june	symphony	
1959		

FRANZ JOSEF HAYDN (1732-1809)

symphony no 93

walthamstow   london   cd: decca 417 6202/436 2902
30 april-   philharmonic   *excerpts*
1 may   cd: decca 436 7532
1987

symphony no 94 "surprise"

london   london   cd: decca 411 8972/436 2902/
9-10   philharmonic   436 6002/436 6172
december
1983

symphony no 95

london   london   cd: decca 417 3302/436 2902
23 october   philharmonic
1985

symphony no 96 "miracle"

london   london   lp: decca SXDL 7544
25-30   philharmonic   lp: london (usa) LDR 71044
march   cd: decca 417 5212/436 2902
1981

haydn **symphony no 97**

walthamstow   london   cd: decca 433 3962/436 2902
17 october   philharmonic
1989

symphony no 98

watford   london   cd: decca 433 3962/436 2902
21 february   philharmonic
1991

symphony no 99

walthamstow   london   cd: decca 417 6202/436 2902
26-27   philharmonic
november
1986

symphony no 100 "military"

london   london   lp: decca LXT 2984
23 april   philharmonic   lp: london (usa) LL 1043/CM 9106
1954

london   london   cd: decca 411 8972/436 2902/
27-28   philharmonic   436 6002/436 6172
november
1983

symphony no 101 "clock"

london   london   lp: decca SXDL 7544
25-30   philharmonic   lp: london (usa) LDR 71044
march   cd: decca 417 5212/436 2902
1981

haydn **symphony no 102**

cologne 23 april 1951	wdr orchestra	unpublished radio broadcast
london 20-26 november 1951	london philharmonic	lp: decca LXT 2984/LW 5288 lp: london (usa) LL 1043/CM 9106 *issued on cd by priceless*
london 8-16 december 1981	london philharmonic	lp: decca SXDL 7570 lp: london (usa) LDR 71070 cd: decca 414 6732/436 2902

symphony no 103 "drum roll"

london 29-31 august 1949	london philharmonic	78: decca AX 333-335 lp: decca LX 3018/ACL 107 lp: london (usa) LL 557/LPS 124
london 8-16 december 1981	london philharmonic	lp: decca SXDL 7570 lp: london (usa) LDR 71070 cd: decca 414 6732/436 2902

haydn symphony no 104 "london"

london 19-23 may 1985	london philharmonic	cd: decca 417 3302/ 436 2902

die jahreszeiten

chicago may 1992	chicago so and chorus ziesak heilmann pape	cd: decca 436 8402

die schöpfung

chicago 9-12 november 1981	chicago so and chorus burrowes greenberg wohlers moll nimsgern	lp: decca D262 D2 lp: london (usa) LDR 72011 cd: decca 430 4732 *excerpts* cd: decca 430 7392
chicago 29 october- 2 november 1993	chicago so and chorus ziesak lippert pape scharinger	cd: decca 443 4452

GUSTAV HOLST (1874-1934)

the planets

london 14-15 february 1978	london philharmonic	lp: decca SET 628/417 2681 lp: london (usa) CS 7110 lp: mobile fidelity MFSLI 510 cd: decca 414 5672/425 1522/430 4472/ 430 6352/440 3182/444 5492 *jupiter only* cd: decca 440 6382/443 9362/461 2862

ARTHUR HONEGGER (1892-1955)

pacific 231

cologne 23 april 1951	wdr orchestra	unpublished radio broadcast

ENGELBERT HUMPERDINCK (1854-1921)

hänsel und gretel

vienna 27 february- 3 march 1978	vienna philharmonic wiener sängerknaben popp fassbänder hamari schlemm berry	lp: decca D131 D2 lp: london (usa) OSA 12112 cd: decca 455 0632 *excerpts* cd: decca 448 8802/460 8452/460 9822 *recording completed in june 1978*
vienna 5-6 june 1980	vienna philharmonic wiener sängerknaben gruberova fassbänder dernesch jurinac prey	vhs video: decca 071 1023

ZOLTAN KODALY (1882-1967)

dances of galanta
london	london	lp: decca LXT 2771/ACL 75/
11-12	philharmonic	ECM 519/ECS 519
november		lp: london (usa) LL 709
1952		cd: decca 425 9692

peacock variations
london	london	lp: decca LXT 2878/ECM 519/ECS 519
26 april-	philharmonic	lp: london (usa) LL 1020
3 may		cd: decca 425 9692
1954		

vienna	vienna	cd: decca 452 8532
19-22	philharmonic	
april		
1996		

psalmus hungaricus
london	london	lp: decca LXT 2878/ECM 533/ECS 533
26 april-	philharmonic	lp: london (usa) LL 1020
3 may	lpo choir	
1954	mcalpine	
	sung in english	

chicago	chicago so	cd: chicago symphony orchestra CSO 9012
18-20	and chorus	
november		
1982		

budapest	budapest	cd: decca 458 9292
june	festival	
1997	orchestra	
	hungarian	
	choirs	
	daroczy	

kodaly **hary janos, concert suite**

munich may 1949	bavarian state orchestra	78: dg LM 68 392-68 394 lp: decca (usa) DL 9518
cologne 23 april 1951	wdr orchestra	unpublished radio broadcast
london 21-23 february 1955	london philharmonic	lp: decca LXT 5059/LW 5256/ ACL 75/ECM 519/ECS 519 lp: london (usa) LL 1230/CM 9132 lp: turnabout TV 34618 cd: decca 425 9692
cologne 16 february 1968	wdr orchestra	unpublished radio broadcast
chicago november 1993	chicago so	cd: decca 443 4442
vienna april 1995	vienna philharmonic	vhs video: decca 071 1843

FRANZ LISZT (1811-1886)

a faust symphony

chicago 20-21 january 1986	chicago so and chorus jerusalem	cd: decca 417 3992/466 7512

piano concerto no 1

walthamstow 7-10 july 1986	london philharmonic bolet	decca unpublished

piano concerto no 2

walthamstow 7-10 july 1986	london philharmonic bolet	decca unpublished

mephisto waltz no 1/episodes from lenau's faust

paris may 1975	orchestre de paris	lp: decca SXL 6709 lp: london (usa) CS 6925 cd: decca 417 5132
chicago november 1993	chicago so	cd: decca 443 4442

liszt **hungarian rhapsody no 2 in d minor**

chicago november 1993	chicago so	cd: decca 443 4442

festklänge

london 4-6 april 1977	london philharmonic	lp: decca SXL 6863 lp: london (usa) CS 7084 cd: decca 417 5132
chicago 21 may 1977	chicago so	cd: chicago symphony orchestra CSO 892892

prometheus

london 4-6 april 1977	london philharmonic	lp: decca SXL 6863 lp: london (usa) CS 7084 cd: decca 417 5132/466 7512 *recording completed on 30 june 1977*

tasso

paris 29 may- 1 june 1974	orchestre de paris	lp: decca SXL 6709 lp: london (usa) CS 6925 cd: decca 417 5132

liszt **les préludes**

london 4-6 april 1977	london philharmonic	lp: decca SXL 6863 lp: london (usa) CS 7084 cd: decca 417 5132/461 2862/466 7512
munich 31 december 1980	bavarian radio orchestra	unpublished radio broadcast
salzburg 8 june 1992	chicago so	cd: decca 436 8392

von der wiege bis zum grabe

paris june 1974	orchestre de paris	lp: decca SXL 6709 lp: london (usa) CS 6925

WITOLD LUTOSLAWSKI (1913-1994)

symphony no 3

chicago 29 september- 1 october 1983	chicago so	cd: chicago symphony orchestra CD 9010

GUSTAV MAHLER (1860-1911)

symphony no 1

london   london so   lp: decca LXT 6113/SXL 6113/7BB 173-177
17 january-   lp: london (usa) CM 9401/CS 6401/CSP 7
5 february   cd: decca 417 7012/425 0052/448 9212
1964   *second movement*
                                     lp: decca SPA 362

salzburg   vienna   unpublished radio broadcast
16 august   philharmonic
1964

chicago   chicago so   lp: decca 411 7311
10-11   cd: decca 411 7312/430 8042
october
1983

symphony no 2 "resurrection"

london   london so   lp: decca MET 325-326/SET 325-326/
21-26   lso chorus   7BB 173-177/DJB 2001
may   harper   lp: london (usa) CMA 7217/CSA 2217/
1966   watts   CSP 7/JL 42006
                                     cd: decca 425 0052/448 9212

chicago   chicago so   lp: decca D229 D2
5-8   and chorus   lp: london (usa) LDR 72006
may   buchanan   cd: decca 410 2022/430 8042
1980   zakai

mahler **symphony no 3**
london	london so	lp: decca SET 385-386/7BB 173-177/414 2541
1-6	lso chorus	lp: london (usa) CSA 2223/CSP 7
january	watts	cd: decca 414 2542
1968		

chicago	chicago so	lp: decca D281 D2
13-16	and chorus	lp: london (usa) LDR 72014
november	dernesch	cd: decca 414 2682/430 8042
1982		*recording completed on 29 march 1983*

symphony no 4
amsterdam	concertgebouw	lp: decca LXT 5638/SXL 2276/
20-21	orchestra	7BB 183-187
february	stahlman	lp: london (usa) CM 9217/CM 9286/
1961		CM 9781/CS 6217/CS 6781/CSP 7
		cd: decca 417 7452/430 8042/458 3832
		first movement
		lp: decca SPA 362

new york	new york	cd: new york philharmonic mahler
13 january	philharmonic	edition
1962	seefried	

chicago	chicago so	lp: decca 410 1881
28-29	kanawa	cd: decca 410 1882/430 8042
march		
1983		

symphony no 5
chicago	chicago so	lp: decca SET 471-472/7BB 178-182/
26 march-		414 3211
7 april		lp: london (usa) CSA 2228/CSP 7
1970		cd: decca 414 3212/430 4432/430 6352/
		430 8042/458 3832
		adagietto
		lp: decca SPA 127/SPA 362
		lp: london (usa) CS 6730

tokyo	chicago so	vhs video: sony SHV 46377
26 march		laserdisc: sony SLV 46377
1986		

vienna	chicago so	cd: decca 433 3292
30 november		
1993		

mahler **symphony no 6**

chicago 26 march- 7 april 1970	chicago so	lp: decca SET 469-470/7BB 178-182 lp: london (usa) CSA 2227/CSP 7 cd: decca 414 6742/425 0402/430 8042

symphony no 7

chicago 12-14 may 1971	chicago so	lp: decca SET 518-519/7BB 178-182 lp: london (usa) CSA 2231/CSP 7 cd: decca 414 6752/425 0412/430 8042

symphony no 8 "symphony of a thousand"

vienna 30 august- 1 september 1971	chicago so vienna opera chorus wiener singverein wiener sängerknaben harper popp auger minton kollo shirley-quirk talvela	lp: decca SET 534-535/7BB 183-187 lp: london (usa) OSA 1295/CSP 7 cd: decca 414 4932/430 8042/ 418 2932/460 9722 *excerpts* lp: decca SPA 362

mahler symphony no 9

london 28 april- 11 may 1967	london so	lp: decca MET 360-361/SET 360-361/ 7BB 183-187/410 2641 lp: london (usa) CSA 2220/CSP 7 cd: decca 430 2472
chicago 3-10 may 1982	chicago so	lp: decca D274 D2 lp: london (usa) LDR 72012 cd: decca 410 0122/430 8042

das lied von der erde

cologne 30 may 1960	wdr orchestra töpper mccracken	unpublished radio broadcast
chicago 8-9 may 1972	chicago so minton kollo	lp: decca SET 555/414 0661 lp: london (usa) OS 26292 cd: decca 414 0662
amsterdam 4-10 december 1992	concertgebouw orchestra lipovsek moser	cd: decca 440 3142

kindertotenlieder

paris 5 may 1965	orchestre national fischer-dieskau	unpublished radio broadcast

mahler **four songs from des knaben wunderhorn (verlor'ne müh'; das irdische leben; rheinlegendchen; wo die schönen trompeten blasen)**
chicago	chicago so	lp: decca SET 471-472/SXL 6679
26 march-	minton	lp: london (usa) CSA 2228/OS 26195
7 april		cd: decca 414 0662/414 6752
1970		

lieder eines fahrenden gesellen
chicago	chicago so	lp: decca SET 469-470/SXL 6679
26 march	minton	lp: london (usa) CSA 2227/OS 26195
1970		cd: decca 414 6742
		excerpts
		lp: decca SPA 362

PIETRO MASCAGNI (1863-1945)

cavalleria rusticana, excerpt (voi lo sapete)
chicago	lyric opera	lp: decca LXT 5326
10 november	orchestra	lp: london (usa) A 5320/LL 1626
1956	simionato	cd: decca 448 1542

FELIX MENDELSSOHN-BARTHOLDY (1809-1847)

symphony no 3 "scotch"
london	london so	lp: decca LXT 2768/ACL 149/
14-15		ECM 527/ECS 527
november		lp: london (usa) LL 708
1952		

chicago	chicago so	vhs video: decca 071 1103
23-24		
october		
1979		

chicago	chicago so	lp: decca 411 6651
8-9		cd: decca 411 6652
april		
1985		

mendelssohn **symphony no 4 "italian"**

tel aviv
21-25
may
1958
	israel
	philharmonic
		lp: decca LXT 5477/SXL 2067/
		    ADD 121/SDD 121
		lp: london (usa) CM 9065/CS 6065/
		    STS 15008
		cd: decca 433 0232

chicago 1-2 june 1976	chicago so	vhs video: decca 071 1103
chicago 9 april 1985	chicago so	lp: decca 411 6651 cd: decca 411 6652
munich 28 january 1992	bavarian radio orchestra	unpublished video recording
vienna 6-7 february 1993	vienna philharmonic	cd: decca 440 4762/448 9452

violin concerto

chicago 23-24 october 1979	chicago so chung	vhs video: decca 071 1103

a midsummer night's dream, overture

chicago 1 may 1976	chicago so	cd: chicago symphony orchestra CSO 892892
chicago 1-2 june 1976	chicago so	laserdisc: jvc JHC 0121

WOLFGANG AMADEUS MOZART (1756-1791)
symphony no 25

london 21-22 april 1954	london so	lp: decca LXT 2946/LW 5301/ ECM 591/ECS 591 lp: london (usa) LL 1034/R 23238
chicago 26-28 april 1984	chicago so	cd: chicago symphony orchestra CD 9010

symphony no 35 "haffner"

tokyo 26 march 1986	chicago so	vhs video: sony SHV 46377 laserdisc: sony SLV 46377

symphony no 38 "prague"

london 21-22 april 1954	london so	lp: decca LXT 2946/ECM 591/ECS 591 lp: london (usa) LL 1034/R 23238
cologne 30 may 1960	wdr orchestra	unpublished radio broadcast
chicago 20 april 1982	chicago so	lp: decca SXDL 7588 lp: london (usa) LDR 71088 cd: decca 417 7822/448 9242

symphony no 39

chicago 17-20 april 1982	chicago so	lp: decca SXDL 7588 lp: london (usa) LDR 71088 cd: decca 417 7822/448 9242

symphony no 40

frankfurt 12-16 april 1984	chamber orchestra of europe	lp: decca 414 3341 cd: decca 414 3342/430 4372/ 430 6352/448 9242

mozart **symphony no 41 "jupiter"**
cologne 25 june 1956	wdr orchestra	unpublished radio broadcast
chicago 18 may 1978	chicago so	cd: chicago symphony orchestra CSO 9012
frankfurt 12-16 april 1984	chamber orchestra of europe	lp: decca 414 3341 cd: decca 414 3342/430 4372/448 9242

piano concerto no 17
london 25 february 1990	covent garden orchestra perahia	unpublished radio broadcast *music performance research centre*

piano concerto no 20
cologne 21 january 1952	wdr orchestra solti, pianist and conductor	lp: replica RPL 2471
walthamstow 30 june 1989	english chamber orchestra solti, pianist and conductor	cd: decca 430 2322

piano concerto no 24
london march 1985	london philharmonic larrocha	decca unpublished *sessions may have been scheduled but not taken place or not been completed*

piano concerto no 25
london 18-22 december 1977	london philharmonic larrocha	lp: decca SXL 6887/417 4621 lp: london (usa) CS 7109 cd: decca 461 3462

mozart piano concerto no 26 "coronation"
london	london	decca unpublished
march	philharmonic	*sessions may have been scheduled but not taken place*
1985	larrocha	*or not been completed*

piano concerto no 27
london	london	lp: decca SXL 6887/417 4621
18-22	philharmonic	cd: decca 461 3462
december	larrocha	
1977		

concerto for two pianos
london	english	cd: decca 430 2322
16 june	chamber	vhs video: teldec 9031 707773
1989	orchestra	
	barenboim	
	solti, pianist	
	and conductor	

concerto for three pianos
london	english	cd: decca 430 2322
16 june	chamber	vhs video: teldec 9031 707773
1989	orchestra	
	barenboim	
	schiff	
	solti, pianist	
	and conductor	

violin concerto no 4
cologne	wdr orchestra	unpublished radio broadcast
23 april	grumiaux	
1951		

serenade no 13 "eine kleine nachtmusik"
tel aviv	israel	45: decca SEC 5007
21-25	philharmonic	lp: decca LXT 5472/SXL 2046
may		lp: london (usa) CM 9010/CS 6066/
1958		STS 15141
		cd: decca 436 5222

adagio and fugue in c minor
chicago	chicago so	cd: chicago symphony orchestra
6 november		CSO 892892
1976		

mozart **requiem**
vienna	vienna	cd: decca 433 6882
5 december	philharmonic	vhs video: decca 071 1393
1991	vienna opera	*performed in saint stephen's cathedral on the*
	concert chorus	*200th anniversary of mozart's death*
	auger	
	bartoli	
	cole	
	pape	

mass in c minor
vienna	vienna	cd: decca 433 7492
december	philharmonic	
1990	vienna opera	
	concert chorus	
	norberg-schulz	
	otter	
	heilmann	
	pape	

cosi fan tutte
london	london	lp: decca SET 575-578/D56 D4
1-17	philharmonic	lp: london (usa) OSA 1442
july	covent garden	cd: decca 430 1012
1973	chorus	*excerpts*
	lorengar	lp: decca SET 595/414 6121
	berganza	cd: decca 421 3112/421 8992/443 5912
	berbié	
	davies	
	krause	
	bacquier	
london	chamber	cd: decca 444 1742
3-5	orchestra	
may	of europe	
1994	london voices	
	fleming	
	otter	
	scarabelli	
	lopardo	
	bär	
	pertusi	

294
mozart **don giovanni**

london	covent garden	unpublished radio broadcast
9 february	orchestra	*excerpts*
1962	and chorus	cd: arkadia CD 575/CDHP 575
	gencer	
	jurinac	
	freni	
	r.lewis	
	siepi	
	evans	
	ward	
london	london	lp: decca D162 D4
4 october-	philharmonic	lp: london (usa) OSA 1444
8 november	london opera	cd: decca 425 1692
1978	chorus	*excerpts*
	m.price	lp: decca GRV 23
	sass	cd: decca 430 1262
	popp	
	burrows	
	weikl	
	bacquier	
	moll	
london	london	cd: decca 455 5002
26 september-	philharmonic	*excerpts*
7 october	london voices	cd: decca 466 0652
1996	fleming	*also unpublished video recording of piano*
	murray	*rehearsals*
	groop	
	lippert	
	terfel	
	pertusi	
	luperi	

don giovanni, overture

london	covent garden	unpublished radio broadcast
undated	orchestra	

mozart **die entführung aus dem serail**

vienna	vienna	lp: decca 417 4021
5-8	philharmonic	cd: decca 417 4022
november	vienna opera	*excerpts*
1984	chorus	cd: decca 430 1212/448 2492
	gruberova	*recording completed in december 1984*
	battle	
	winbergh	
	zednik	
	talvela	
	quadflieg	
london	covent garden	vhs video: nvc arts 0603 187733
1987	orchestra	
	and chorus	
	nielsen	
	watson	
	van der welt	
	magnusson	
	moll	
	tobias	

idomeneo

salzburg	vienna	unpublished radio broadcast
27 july	philharmonic	
1951	vienna opera	
	chorus	
	güden	
	lawrence	
	schock	
	holm	
	cordes-dermota	
	böhme	

mozart **le nozze di figaro**

london 11 june 1963	covent garden orchestra and chorus ligabue freni berganza gobbi evans	unpublished radio broadcast *music performance research centre*
paris 1980	paris opéra orchestra and chorus janowitz popp stade van dam bacquier	vhs video: lyric (usa) 1096 vhs video: sony (japan) 002M 7015-7016 laserdisc: dreamlife DMLB 29

london
29 may-
8 june
1981
	london
	philharmonic
	london opera
	chorus
	kanawa
	popp
	stade
	allen
	ramey
		lp: decca D267 D4
		lp: london (usa) LDR 74001
		cd: decca 410 1502
		excerpts
		lp: decca 417 2011
		cd: decca 417 2012/417 3952/417 6452/
		    425 8512/430 1112/430 4982/
		    433 0682/433 3232/433 8222/
		    436 2862/436 4612/436 4622/
		    436 4722/436 7532/440 2032/
		    440 4012/440 9472/443 5912/
		    443 5942/443 5952/444 6152/
		    448 1352/448 2512/448 7132/460 9822
		*overture recorded on 8 december 1981; excerpts
		also issued on lp by readers digest*

le nozze di figaro, excerpt (dove sono)

london 22-23 february 1968	covent garden orchestra carlyle	lp: decca SET 392-393 lp: london (usa) OSA 1276
london 16-21 december 1996	london so fleming	cd: decca 455 7602

mozart **le nozze di figaro, excerpt (voi che sapete)**
chicago	lyric opera	lp: decca LXT 5326
10 november	orchestra	lp: london (usa) A 5320/LL 1626
1956	simionato	cd: decca 448 1542

le nozze di figaro, excerpt (porgi amor)
london	london so	cd: decca 455 7602
16-21	fleming	
december		
1996		

die zauberflöte
frankfurt	hessischer	lp: melodram MEL 044
1955	rundfunk	
	orchestra	
	and chorus	
	grümmer	
	köth	
	steffek	
	kozub	
	frick	
	ambrosius	
salzburg	vienna	unpublished radio broadcast
2 august	philharmonic	*excerpts*
1956	vienna opera	cd: orfeo C394 201B/C408 955R
	chorus	
	grümmer	
	köth	
	rothenberger	
	dermota	
	berry	
	frick	
	schöffler	
vienna	vienna	lp: decca SET 479-481
26 september-	philharmonic	lp: london (usa) OSA 1397
8 october	vienna opera	cd: decca 414 5682
1969	chorus	*excerpts*
	lorengar	lp: decca SET 527
	deutekom	lp: london (usa) OS 26257
	holm	cd: decca 421 3022/433 4412/458 2132
	burrows	
	prey	
	talvela	
	fischer-dieskau	

mozart die zauberflöte/concluded

vienna	vienna	cd: decca 433 2102
1-9	philharmonic	*excerpts*
may	vienna opera	cd: decca 433 6672
1990	chorus	*recording completed 10-15 december 1990*
	ziesak	
	jo	
	leitner	
	heilmann	
	m.kraus	
	moll	
	schmidt	
salzburg	vienna	unpublished video recording
july	philharmonic	
1991	vienna opera	
	concert chorus	

die zauberflöte, overture

viersen	wdr orchestra	unpublished radio broadcast
18september		
1950		
london	covent garden	unpublished radio orchestra
undated	orchestra	

piano quartet no 1

frankfurt	members of	lp: decca 417 1901
12-14	melos quartet	cd: decca 417 1902
april	solti, piano	
1984		

piano quartet no 2

london	members of	lp: decca 417 1901
26-27	melos quartet	cd: decca 417 1902
june	solti, piano	
1985		

violin sonata k454

zürich	kulenkampff	78: decca AK 2101-2103/K 23056-23058
july	solti, piano	78: london (usa) EDA 108
1948		lp: decca ACL 211/ECM 831
		lp: decca (germany) KD 11020
		lp: london (usa) CM 9507/R 23214
		cd: urania URN 22.112

MODEST MUSSORGSKY (1839-1881)
pictures from an exhibition, arranged by ravel

chicago 7-8 may 1980	chicago so	lp: decca SXDL 7520 lp: london (usa) LDR 10040 cd: decca 400 0512/ 417 7542/ 430 4462/430 6852
tokyo march 1986	chicago so	vhs video: sony SHV 46373 laserdisc: sony SLV 46373 *includes introductory talk by solti*

night on bare mountain

berlin 2-5 june 1959	berlin philharmonic	lp: decca SPA 257 lp: london (usa) CS 6944/JL 41051 cd: polygram (japan) POCL 2013

london
31 january-
3 february
1966
	london so	lp: decca LXT 6263/SXL 6263
		lp: london (usa) CM 9503/CM 9785/
		    CS 6503/CS 6785
		cd: decca 417 6892/417 7232/450 0172/
		    455 6322/460 9772

songs and dances of death

chicago february 1995	chicago so aleksashkin	cd: decca 458 9192

boris godunov

new york 6 april 1963	metropolitan opera orchestra and chorus elias gedda cassel franke hines tozzi alvary	unpublished met broadcast

khovantschina, dance of the persian slaves

berlin 2-5 june 1959	berlin philharmonic	lp: decca SPA 257 lp: london (usa) CS 6944/JL 41051 cd: polygram (japan) POCL 2013

mussorgsky **khovantschina, prelude**

berlin 2-5 june 1959	berlin philharmonic	lp: decca SPA 257 lp: london (usa) CS 6944/JL 41051 cd: polygram (japan) POCL 2013

london
31 january-
3 february
1966
	london so	lp: decca LXT 6263/SXL 6263
		lp: london (usa) CM 9503/CM 9785/
		    CS 6503/CS 6785
		cd: decca 417 6892/417 7232/450 0172/
		    455 6322/460 9772/460 9882

chicago 17-18 october 1977	chicago so	unpublished video recording

CARL NIELSEN (1864-1931)
symphony no 1

chicago 26 may 1976	chicago so	cd: chicago symphony orchestra CSO 892898

JACQUES OFFENBACH (1819-1880)
gaité parisienne, arranged by rosenthal

london 18-27 may 1960	covent garden orchestra	lp: decca LXT 5642/SXL 2280/JB 12 lp: london (usa) CM 9285/CS 6216/ CS 6780/JL 41029 cd: decca 448 9422

barcarolle/les contes d'hoffmann

london
18-21
june
1958
	covent garden
	orchestra
		lp: victor LM 2313/LSC 2313/RB 16172/
		    RB 6542/SB 2058/SB 6542/
		    VIC 1119/VICS 1119
		lp: decca SPA 347
		lp: london (usa) CS 6753
		cd: decca 433 6212

CARL ORFF (1895-1982)
antigonae

munich 12 january 1951	bavarian state orchestra and chorus goltz schech haefliger uhde kusche	cd: orfeo C407 952I

AMILCARE PONCHIELLI (1834-1886)

dance of the hours/la gioconda
london	covent garden	lp: victor LM 2313/LSC 2313/RB 16172/
18-21	orchestra	SB 2058/VIC 1119/VICS 1119
june		lp: decca SPA 347
1958		lp: london (usa) CS 6753
		cd: decca 433 6212

la gioconda, excerpt (l'amo come il fulgor!)
chicago	lyric opera	lp: decca LXT 5326
10 november	orchestra	lp: london (usa) A 5320/LL 1626
1956	tebaldi	cd: decca 448 1542
	simionato	

SERGE PROKOFIEV (1891-1953)

symphony no 1 "classical"
chicago	chicago so	unpublished video recording
17-18		
october		
1977		

chicago	chicago so	lp: decca SXDL 7587
11 may		lp: london (usa) LDR 71087
1982		cd: decca 410 2002/430 4462/
		430 6352/430 7312

piano concerto no 3
cologne	wdr orchestra	unpublished radio broadcast
3 november	magaloff	
1952		

romeo and juliet, excerpts from the ballet
chicago	chicago so	lp: decca SXDL 7587
10-11		lp: london (usa) LDR 71087
may		cd: decca 410 2002/430 7312
1982		

munich	bavarian radio	laserdisc: pioneer (usa) PLMCB 00591/
10 february	orchestra	24910/PA 90344
1984		

london	covent garden	unpublished radio broadcast
25 february	orchestra	*music performance research centre*
1990		

GIACOMO PUCCINI (1858-1924)

la bohème

walthamstow
25 july–
3 august
1974
	london
	philharmonic
	alldis choir
	caballé
	blegen
	domingo
	milnes
	raimondi
	sardinero
		lp: victor ARL2-0371/ARD2-0371/
		  VLS 45760
		cd: rca/bmg RD 80371/RCD 20371
		excerpts
		lp: victor RL 04199/RL 14265/
		  CRL2-4199/AFL1-4265
		cd: rca/bmg RD 86211/GD 84265/
		  GD 60841/GD 60866/07863 562112/
		  09026 613562/09026 614402/
		  09026 617252/74321 178972/
		  74321 212732/74321 242822/
		  74321 258172

tosca

walthamstow 2-3 february 1984	national philharmonic orchestra welsh national opera chorus kanawa aragall nucci	lp: decca 414 5971 cd: decca 414 5972 *excerpts* cd: decca 421 6112/430 7112 *recording completed 15-30 may 1984*

turandot

cologne may 1956	wdr orchestra and chorus goltz stich-randall hopf schiebener schirp *sung in german*	unpublished radio broadcast

SERGEI RACHMANINOV (1873-1943)

piano concerto no 2

london 16-18 june 1958	london so katchen	lp: decca LXT 5490/SXL 2076/ADD 181/ SDD 181/SPA 505 lp: london (usa) CM 9064/CS 6064/ STS 15046/STS 15086 cd: decca 417 8802/436 5212/448 6042

MAURICE RAVEL (1875-1937)

boléro

chicago 24-25 may 1976	chicago so	lp: decca SXL 6813 lp: london (usa) CS 7033 cd: decca 417 7042/430 4442/430 6352

daphnis et chloé, second suite

chicago 15-20 january 1987	chicago so	cd: chicago symphony orchestra CD 9012

le tombeau de couperin

chicago 7-8 may 1980	chicago so	lp: decca SXDL 7520 lp: london (usa) LDR 10040 cd: decca 400 0512/430 4442/430 6352

la valse

chicago 23 october 1976	chicago so	cd: chicago symphony orchestra CSO 892892

GIOACHINO ROSSINI (1792-1868)

la boutique fantasque, arranged by respighi

tel aviv
april
1957
	israel
	philharmonic
		lp: decca LXT 5341/SXL 2007/ADD 109/
		    SDD 109/SPA 376
		lp: london (usa) LL 1715/CM 9202/
		    CS 6005/STS 15005
		cd: decca 425 5092/448 9422
		excerpts
		45: decca CEP 547/SEC 5015
		lp: decca SPA 127

l' assiedo di corinto, overture

chicago 5-6 december 1978	chicago so	unpublished video recording

il barbiere di siviglia, overture

london 23-25 february 1955	london philharmonic	45: decca CEP 653 lp: decca LW 5207 lp: london (usa) LD 9207
chicago 23 may 1972	chicago so	lp: decca SXL 6684 lp: london (usa) CS 6800 cd: decca 460 9822
chicago 5-6 december 1978	chicago so	laserdisc: decca 071 1071

rossini **la gazza ladra, overture**
chicago   chicago so   laserdisc: decca 071 1071
5-6
december
1978

guillaume tell, overture

geneva   world peace   cd: decca 448 9012
5 july   orchestra   vhs video: decca 071 1833
1995

l'italiana in algeri, overture
london   london   45: decca CEP 653
23-25   philharmonic   lp: decca LW 5207
february
1955

london   covent garden   lp: victor LM 2313/LSC 2313/RB 16172/
18-21   orchestra   SB 2058/VIC 1119/VICS 1119
june   lp: decca SPA 347
1958   lp: london (usa) CS 6753

chicago   chicago so   laserdisc: decca 071 1071
5-6
december
1978

la scala di seta, overture
chicago   chicago so   laserdisc: decca 071 1071
5-6
december
1958

semiramide, overture
london   covent garden   lp: victor LM 2313/LSC 2313/RB 16172/
18-21   orchestra   SB 2058/VIC 1119/VICS 1119
june   lp: decca SPA 347
1958   lp: london (usa) CS 6753

chicago   chicago so   laserdisc: decca 071 1071
5-6
december
1978

CAMILLE SAINT-SAENS (1835-1921)

samson et dalila, excerpt (mon coeur s'ouvre a ta voix)

chicago	lyric opera	lp: decca LXT 5326
10 november	orchestra	lp: london (usa) A 5320/LL 1626
1956	simionato	cd: decca 448 1542
	sung in italian	

ARNOLD SCHOENBERG (1874-1951)

moses und aaron

london	covent garden	unpublished radio broadcast
28 june	orchestra	*music performance research centre*
1965	and chorus	
	r.lewis	
	robinson	

chicago	chicago so	lp: decca 414 2641
23 april-	and chorus	cd: decca 414 2642
1 may	langridge	
1984	haugland	

variations for orchestra

chicago	chicago so	lp: london (usa) CS 6984
14 may		cd: decca 425 0082
1975		

FRANZ SCHUBERT (1797-1828)
symphony no 5

tel aviv may 1958	israel philharmonic	lp: decca LXT 5477/SXL 2067/ 　　ADD 121/SDD 121 lp: london (usa) CM 9065/CS 6065/ 　　STS 15008
vienna 12-14 september 1984	vienna philharmonic	lp: decca 414 3711 cd: decca 414 3712/448 9272

symphony no 6

chicago 5-6 december 1978	chicago so	laserdisc: jvc JHC 0121

symphony no 8 "unfinished"

cologne 9 september 1955	wdr orchestra	unpublished radio broadcast
cologne 16 february 1968	wdr orchestra	unpublished radio broadcast
chicago 5-6 december 1978	chicago so	laserdisc: jvc JHC 0121
vienna 12-14 september 1984	vienna philharmonic	lp: decca 414 3711 cd: decca 414 3712/448 9272

symphony no 9 "great"

viersen 18 september 1950	wdr orchestra	unpublished radio orchestra
vienna 23-25 june 1981	vienna philharmonic	lp: decca SXDL 7557 lp: london (usa) LDR 71057 cd: decca 400 0822/448 9272/460 3112

schubert **wanderer fantasy for piano and orchestra, arranged by liszt**

walthamstow 7-10 july 1986	london philharmonic bolet	cd: decca 425 6892/430 7362/458 3612

lieder: abschied; in der ferne/schwanengesang

zürich 25 june 1947	lichtegg solti, piano	78: decca K 2172

ROBERT SCHUMANN (1810-1856)

symphony no 1 "spring"

vienna 10-13 september 1969	vienna philharmonic	lp: decca SXL 6486 lp: london (usa) CS 6696/CSA 2310 cd: decca 417 7872/448 9302

symphony no 2

vienna 10-13 september 1967	vienna philharmonic	lp: decca SXL 6487 lp: london (usa) CS 6697/CSA 2310 cd: decca 417 7872/448 9302

schumann **symphony no 3 "rhenish"**

vienna	vienna	lp: decca LXT 6356/SXL 6356/VIV 46
22-23	philharmonic	lp: london (usa) CS 6582/CSA 2310
november		cd: decca 417 7992/448 9302
1967		

symphony no 4

vienna	vienna	lp: decca LXT 6356/SXL 6356/VIV 46
22-23	philharmonic	lp: london (usa) CS 6582/CSA 2310
november		cd: decca 417 7992/448 9302
1967		

julius cäsar, overture

vienna	vienna	lp: decca SXL 6487
10-13	philharmonic	lp: london (usa) CS 6697/CSA 2310
september		cd: decca 417 7872/448 9302
1969		

overture, scherzo and finale

vienna	vienna	lp: decca SXL 6486
10-13	philharmonic	lp: london (usa) CS 6696/CSA 2310
september		cd: decca 448 9302
1969		

DIMITRI SHOSTAKOVICH (1906-1975)

symphony no 1
chicago 17-18 october 1977	chicago so	unpublished video recording
amsterdam 18-21 september 1991	concertgebouw orchestra	cd: decca 436 4692

symphony no 5
vienna 6-7 february 1993	vienna philharmonic	cd: decca 440 4762

symphony no 8
chicago 2-4 february 1989	chicago so	cd: decca 425 6752

symphony no 9
vienna 5-6 may 1990	vienna philharmonic	cd: decca 430 5052
new york 13 june 1994	orchestra of the solti orchestral project	cd: decca 444 4582

shostakovich **symphony no 10**
chicago   chicago so   cd: decca 433 0732
october
1990

symphony no 13 "babi yar"
chicago   chicago so   cd: decca 444 7912
23-26   and chorus
february   alexaschkin
1995   hopkins

symphony no 15
chicago   chicago so   cd: decca 458 9192
1996   *also unpublished video recording*

BEDRICH SMETANA (1824-1884)

the bartered bride, overture
new york   orchestra of   cd: decca 444 4582
13 june   the solti
1994   orchestral
                   project

the moldau/ma vlast
munich   bavarian radio   laserdisc: decca 071 1071
31 december   orchestra
1980

JOHN PHILIP SOUSA (1854-1932)

stars and stripes forever, march
chicago   chicago so   cd: decca 417 3971
27 january
1987

JOHANN STRAUSS (1825-1899)

die fledermaus, overture

london undated	covent garden orchestra	unpublished radio broadcast

RICHARD STRAUSS (1864-1949)

eine alpensinfonie

munich 9-10 september 1979	bavarian radio orchestra	lp: decca SXL 6959 lp: london (usa) CS 7189 cd: decca 414 6762/440 6182

also sprach zarathustra

chicago 13-15 may 1975	chicago so	lp: decca SXL 6749/414 0431 lp: london (usa) CS 6978 cd: decca 414 0432/430 4452/ 430 6352/440 6182
chicago 29 april 1982	chicago so	vhs video: classic (usa) LP 101
berlin 18-20 january 1996	berlin philharmonic	cd: decca 452 6032
munich 1 december 1996	bavarian state orchestra	unpublished video recording *concert for re-opening of prinzregententheater*

strauss **arabella**

vienna 28 may- 9 june 1957	vienna philharmonic vienna opera chorus della casa güden malaniuk dermota london edelmann	lp: decca LXT 5403-5406/SXL 2050-2053/ 　　GOM 571-573/GOS 571-573 lp: london (usa) A 4412/OSA 1404/ 　　SRS 63522 cd: decca 430 3872/458 7002/460 2302 *excerpts* lp: london (usa) CM 5616/OS 25243 cd: decca 440 3502/440 4882/458 2502
london 6 february 1965	covent garden orchestra and chorus della casa carlyle veasey young fischer-dieskau langdon	unpublished radio broadcast *music performance research centre*
london 21 january 1967	covent garden orchestra and chorus carlyle robson reynolds young fischer-dieskau langdon	unpublished radio broadcast
vienna 12-24 january 1977	vienna philharmonic vienna opera chorus janowitz ghazarian mödl kollo weikl rydl	vhs video: decca 071 4053

strauss **ariadne auf naxos**

london 27 november– 6 december 1977	london philharmonic price gruberova troyanos kollo kunz berry	lp: decca D103 D3 lp: london (usa) OSA 13131 cd: decca 430 3842/458 7032/460 2332 *excerpts* lp: decca GRV 10 cd: decca 440 4022/458 2502 *recording completed on 13 february 1978*

daphne, excerpt (ich komm' grünende brüder!)

london 16-21 december 1996	london so fleming	cd: decca 455 7602

don juan

chicago 9 may 1972	chicago so	lp: decca SXL 6749 lp: london (usa) CS 6800/CS 6978 cd: decca 414 0432/430 4452/ 430 6352/440 6182
chicago 17-19 october 1977	chicago so	laserdisc: decca 071 1071
new york 21 june 1994	orchestra of the solti orchestral project	cd: decca 444 4582
munich 1 december 1996	bavarian state orchestra	unpublished video recording *concert for re-opening of prinzregententheater*

strauss **elektra**

vienna 11-19 september 1966	vienna philharmonic vienna opera chorus nilsson collier resnik stolze krause	lp: decca MET 354-355/SET 354-355 lp: london (usa) A 4269/OSA 1269 cd: decca 417 3452/458 7002 *excerpts* lp: decca SET 459 lp: london (usa) OS 26171 cd: decca 458 3982 *preliminary session held on 14 june 1966;* *recording completed in february, june and* *september 1967*
london 23 march 1990	covent garden orchestra and chorus marton secunde lipovsek hale	unpublished radio broadcast *music performance research centre*

elektra, excerpt (allein weh ganz allein!)

munich 2 august 1952	bavarian state orchestra goltz	lp: dg LPM 18 090

elektra, excerpt (ich will nichts hören)

munich 2 august 1952	bavarian state orchestra goltz höngen	lp: dg LPEM 19 038 lp: decca (usa) DL 9723 cd: dg 457 9732

elektra, excerpt (was willst du fremder mensch?)

munich 2 august 1952	bavarian state orchestra goltz frantz	lp: dg LPEM 19 038 lp: decca (usa) DL 9723

strauss **die frau ohne schatten**

london 15 june 1967	covent garden orchestra and chorus hillebrecht borkh resnik king mcintyre	unpublished radio broadcast *music performance research centre*
vienna march- april 1989	vienna philharmonic vienna opera chorus wiener sängerknaben behrens varady runkel domingo van dam	cd: decca 436 2432/458 7002 *recording completed in september 1989 and october 1991*
salzburg august 1992	vienna philharmonic vienna opera concert chorus wiener sängerknaben marton studer lipovsek moser hale	vhs video: decca 071 4253

ein heldenleben

vienna 28-30 march 1977	vienna philharmonic	lp: decca SET 601 lp: london (usa) CS 7083 cd: decca 433 4162/440 6182 *recording completed on 28 march 1978*

strauss **der rosenkavalier**

london december 1959	covent garden orchestra and chorus schwarzkopf jurinac steffek böhme lewis	unpublished radio broadcast *music performance research centre; recording incomplete*
london 30 october 1966	covent garden orchestra and chorus jurinac veasey carlyle langdon	unpublished radio broadcast *music performance research centre*
vienna 31 october- 23 november 1968	vienna philharmonic vienna opera chorus crespin minton donath jungwirth	lp: decca SET 418-421 lp: london (usa) OSA 1435 cd: decca 417 4932/458 7002 *excerpts* lp: decca SET 487 lp: london (usa) OS 26200 cd: decca 458 2502
london december 1984	covent garden orchestra and chorus kanawa howells bonney haugland	vhs video: nvc arts 0630 193913 vhs video: castle CVI 2017

der rosenkavalier, excerpt (da lieg' ich)

london march 1968	covent garden orchestra minton langdon	lp: decca SET 392-393 lp: london (usa) OSA 1276

der rosenkavalier, excerpts (hab' mir's gelobt; ist ein traum kann nicht wirklich sein)

london 25 february 1990	covent garden orchestra lott howells watson	unpublished radio broadcast *music performance research centre*

strauss **salome**

vienna	vienna	lp: decca MET 228-229/SET 228-229
16-21	philharmonic	lp: london (usa) A 4247/OSA 1218
october	nilsson	cd: decca 414 4141/458 7002
1961	hoffman	*excerpts*
	stolze	lp: decca SET 547
	kmentt	lp: london (usa) OS 25991/OS 26169
	wächter	

salome, excerpt (lass mich deinen mund küssen, jokanaan!)

munich	bavarian	unpublished video fragment
1948	state	
	orchestra	
	kupper	
	kronenberg	

dance of the seven veils/salome

berlin	berlin	cd: decca 452 6032
18-20	philharmonic	
january		
1996		

munich	bavarian state	unpublished video recording
1 december	orchestra	*concert for re-opening of prinzregententheater*
1996		

till eulenspiegels lustige streiche

salzburg	vienna	unpublished radio broadcast
16 august	philharmonic	
1964		

chicago	chicago so	lp: decca SXL 6749
13-14		lp: london (usa) CS 6800/CS 6978
may		cd: decca 414 0432/430 4452/
1975		430 6352/440 6182

chicago	chicago so	unpublished video recording
17-19		
october		
1977		

berlin	berlin	cd: decca 452 6032
18-20	philharmonic	
january		
1996		

strauss **tod und verklärung**

chicago 30 september- 1 october 1977	chicago so	cd: chicago symphony orchestra CSO 892892
chicago 17-19 october 1977	chicago so	unpublished video recording
munich 1 december 1996	bavarian state orchestra	unpublished video recording *concert for re-opening of prinzregententheater*

vier letzte lieder

chicago 17-19 october 1977	chicago so popp	unpublished video recording
vienna 8-9 june 1990	vienna philharmonic kanawa	cd: decca 430 5112
manchester 17 june 1990	bbc philharmonic kanawa	vhs video: sony SHV 46379 laserdisc: sony SLV 46379 *documentary programme which also includes* *rehearsal and conversation*

lieder: schlechtes wetter; allerseelen; die nacht; cäcilie; malven;
all mein gedanken; begegnung; morgen; zueignung; madrigal;
muttertändelei; ständchen; hat gesagt bleibt's nicht dabei

walthamstow 12-13 june 1990	kanawa solti, piano	cd: decca 430 5112

lieder with orchestra: zueignung; die nacht; allerseelen; hat gesagt;
muttertändelei; madrigal; ständchen; schlechtes wetter; cäcilie;
begegnung; malven

manchester 17 june 1990	bbc philharmonic knawa	vhs video: sony SHV 46379 laserdisc: sony SLV 46379 *documentary programme which also includes* *rehearsal and conversation*

IGOR STRAVINSKY (1882-1971)
jeu de cartes

cologne 21 january 1952	wdr orchestra	unpublished radio broadcast
chicago november 1993	chicago so	cd: decca 443 7752

oedipus rex

london 8-10 march 1976	london philharmonic alldis choir meyer pears luxon	lp: decca SET 616 lp: london (usa) OSA 1168/OS 26480 cd: decca 430 0012/466 7262

l' oiseau de feu, 1919 suite

cologne 2 june 1958	wdr orchestra	unpublished radio broadcast

berceuse and finale/l' oiseau de feu

london undated	covent garden orchestra	unpublished radio broadcast

petrushka, 1911 version

chicago november 1993	chicago so	cd: decca 443 7752/466 7262

le sacre du printemps

vienna 23-24 september 1963	vienna philharmonic	decca unpublished
chicago 14 may 1974	chicago so	lp: decca SXL 6691/410 1691 lp: london (usa) CS 6885 cd: decca 417 7042
amsterdam 18-21 september 1991	concertgebouw orchestra	cd: decca 436 4692

symphony in c

chicago 1996-1997	chicago so	cd: decca 458 8982

stravinsky **symphony in three movements**   *solti 321*
cologne   wdr orchestra   unpublished radio broadcast
25 june
1956

munich   bavarian radio   unpublished video recording
10-11   orchestra
june
1993

chicago   chicago so   cd: decca 458 8982
1996-1997
symphony of psalms
chicago   chicago so   cd: decca 458 8982
1996-1997

FRANZ VON SUPPE (1819-1895)
light cavalry, overture
london   london   45: decca REP 8019/CEP 555
6-10 april   philharmonic   lp: decca LXT 2589/LW 5003/ACL 87
1951   lp: london (usa) LL 352/LD 9005/B 19064

vienna   vienna   lp: decca LXT 5548/SXL 2174/ADD 194/
3-13   philharmonic   SDD 194/SPA 374
may   lp: london (usa) CM 9040/CS 6146/CS 6779
1959   cd: decca 421 1702/460 9822

london   covent garden   unpublished radio broadcast
undated   orchestra
morning noon and night in vienna, overture
london   london   45: decca REP 8019
6-10 april   philharmonic   lp: decca LXT 2589/LW 5003/ACL 87
1951   lp: london (usa) LL 352/LD 9005/B 19064

vienna   vienna   lp: decca LXT 5548/SXL 2174/ADD 194/
3-13   philharmonic   SDD 194/SPA 374
may   lp: london (usa) CM 9040/CS 6146/CS 6779
1959   cd: decca 421 1702/460 9822
pique dame, overture
london   london   45: decca CEP 555
6-10 april   philharmonic   lp: decca LXT 2589/LW 5004/ACL 87
1951   lp: london (usa) LL 352/LD 9006/B 19064

vienna   vienna   lp: decca LXT 5548/SXL 2174/ADD 194/
3-13   philharmonic   SDD 194/SPA 374
may   lp: london (usa) CM 9040/CS 6146/CS 6779
1959   cd: decca 421 1702

suppé **poet and peasant, overture**

london 6-10 april 1951	london philharmonic	78: decca X 570 lp: decca LXT 2589/LW 5004/ACL 87 lp: london (usa) LL 352/LD 9006/B 1900
vienna 3-13 may 1959	vienna philharmonic	lp: decca LXT 5548/SXL 2174/ADD 194/ SDD 194/SPA 374 lp: london (usa) CM 9040/CS 6146/CS 6779 cd: decca 421 1702/460 9822
london undated	covent garden orchestra	unpublished radio broadcast
munich 31 december 1980	bavarian radio orchestra	unpublished video recording

PIOTR TCHAIKOVSKY (1840-1893)
symphony no 2 "little russian"

paris 22-23 may 1956	conservatoire orchestra	lp: decca LXT 5245/ACL 269/ ECM 703/ECS 703 lp: london (usa) LL 1507/CS 6108/ STS 15120/STS 15141 cd: decca 460 9772

symphony no 4

munich 10 february 1984	bavarian radio orchestra	laserdisc: pioneer (usa) PLMCB 00591/ PA 90344/24910
chicago 5 may 1984	chicago so	lp: decca 414 1921 cd: decca 414 1922/430 7452

symphony no 5

paris 22-26 may 1956	conservatoire orchestra	lp: decca LXT 5241/ACL 165/SPA 223 lp: london (usa) LL 1506/CS 6117/STS 15060
chicago 14-15 may 1975	chicago so	lp: decca SXL 6754 lp: london (usa) CS 6983 cd: decca 417 7232
chicago 28 september- 11 october 1988	chicago so	cd: decca 425 5162

tchaikovsky **symphony no 6 "pathétique"**
chicago			chicago so		lp: decca SXL 6814
24 may						lp: london (usa) CS 7034
1976						cd: decca 417 7082/430 4422/
							430 6352/455 8102

piano concerto no 1
cologne			wdr orchestra	unpublished radio broadcast
2 june			anda
1958

vienna			vienna			lp: decca BR 3042/SXL 2114/
14-17			philharmonic		ADD 191/SDD 191
october			curzon			lp: london (usa) CM 9045/CS 6100/STS 15471
1958						cd: decca 421 6762/436 5322/460 9942

chicago			chicago			vhs video: classic (usa) LP 101
29 april		licad
1982

chicago			chicago so		lp: decca 417 2941
7-8			schiff			cd: decca 417 2942
october
1985

serenade for strings
tel aviv		israel			lp: decca LXT 5472/BR 3067/SXL 2046/
21-25			philharmonic		SWL 8005/SDD 205
may						lp: london (usa) CM 9010/CS 6066/
1958						STS 15141

romeo and juliet, fantasy overture
chicago			chicago so		lp: decca 417 4001
28 january					cd: decca 417 4002/430 4422/430 4462/
1987						430 7072/430 7452/455 8102

1812, ouverture solenelle
chicago			chicago so		lp: decca 417 4001
27 january					cd: decca 417 4002/430 4462/455 8102
1986

casse noisette, ballet suite
chicago			chicago so		lp: decca 417 4001
28 january					cd: decca 417 4002/430 4462/
1986						430 7072/455 8102

swan lake, ballet suite
chicago			chicago so		cd: decca 425 5162/430 7072/455 8102
11 october
1988

tchaikovsky **evgeny onegin**

london	covent garden	unpublished radio broadcast
13 february	orchestra	*music performance research centre*
1971	and chorus	
	cotrubas	
	minton	
	tear	
	braun	
	garrard	

london	covent garden	lp: decca SET 596-598
june-	orchestra	lp: london (usa) OSA 13112
july	and chorus	cd: decca 417 4132
1974	kubiak	vhs video: decca 071 1243
	hamari	*excerpts*
	burrows	lp: decca SET 622
	weikl	
	ghiaurov	

evgeny onegin, excerpt (tatiana's letter scene)

chicago	lyric opera	lp: decca LXT 5326
10 november	orchestra	lp: london (usa) A 5320/LL 1626
1956	tebaldi	cd: decca 448 1542
	sung in italian	

london	london so	cd: decca 455 7602
16-21	fleming	
december		
1996		

MICHAEL TIPPETT (1905-1998)
symphony no 4

chicago	chicago so	lp: decca SXDL 7546/414 0911
29 october		lp: london (usa) LDR 71046
1979		cd: decca 425 6462/433 6682

birthday suite for prince charles

chicago	chicago so	lp: decca SXDL 7546
7 may		lp: london (usa) LDR 71046
1981		cd: decca 425 6462

byzantium, for soprano and orchestra

new york	chicago so	cd: decca 433 6682
15-18	robinson	
april		
1991		

GIUSEPPE VERDI (1813-1901)

aida

rome
24 june-
26 july
1961
	rome opera
	orchestra
	and chorus
	price
	gorr
	vickers
	merrill
		lp: victor LM 6158/RE 25038-25060/
		    LSC 6158/SER 4538-4540
		lp: decca SET 427-429
		lp: london (usa) OSA 1393
		cd: decca 417 4162/460 7652
		excerpts
		lp: victor LM 2616/LSC 2616
		lp: decca JB 81/GRV 10
		cd: decca 421 8602/433 4442/440 4022/
		    440 6542/458 2062/460 8472

new york 7 december 1963	metropolitan opera orchestra and chorus price gorr bergonzi sereni	unpublished met broadcast

aida, excerpt (pur ti riveggo)

munich may 1949	bavarian state orchestra kupper fehenberger *sung in german*	lp: dg LPM 18 009/LPEM 19 027

aida, excerpt (ciel mio padre!)

munich may 1949	bavarian state orchestra kupper reinmar *sung in german*	lp: dg LPM 18 009/LPEM 19 027

aida, excerpt (gloria all' egitto!)

chicago 4-7 november 1989	chicago so and chorus	cd: decca 430 2262

verdi **un ballo in maschera**

rome july 1960- july 1961	santa cecilia orchestra and chorus nilsson stahlman simionato bergonzi macneil	lp: decca LXT 2034-2036/MET 215-217/ SXL 2034-2036/SET 215-217 lp: london (usa) OSA 1328 *excerpts* lp: decca LXT 6013/SXL 6013/GRV 16 lp: london (usa) OS 25714 cd: decca 440 4062/443 9592 cd: grandi voci (italy) GVS 08 *certain aborted sessions in july 1960 involved* *björling and not bergonzi*
london june 1982	national philharmonic orchestra london opera chorus price battle ludwig pavarotti bruson	lp: decca 410 2101 cd: decca 410 2102 *excerpts* cd: decca 425 5292 *recording completed in may 1983*
salzburg 28 july 1990	vienna philharmonic vienna opera concert chorus barstow jo quivar domingo nucci	unpublished video recording

un ballo in maschera, excerpt (posa in pace)

chicago 4-7 november 1989	chicago so and chorus	cd: decca 430 2262

verdi **don carlo**

london	covent garden	lp: decca MET 305-208/SET 305-308
19 june-	orchestra	lp: london (usa) A 4332/OSA 1432
15 july	and chorus	cd: decca 421 1142
1965	tebaldi	*excerpts*
	bumbry	lp: decca GRV 7
	bergonzi	cd: decca 440 4832
	fischer-dieskau	
	ghiaurov	
	talvela	

don carlo, excerpt (si ridesti)

chicago	chicago so	cd: decca 430 2262
4-7	and chorus	
november		
1989		

328
verdi **falstaff**

cologne april 1950	wdr orchestra and chorus cunitz lipp fischer lasser holm reinmar peter *sung in german*	unpublished radio broadcast
rome 6-18 july 1963	rome opera orchestra and chorus ligabue freni elias simionato kraus evans merrill	lp: victor LM 6163/RE 5509-5511/ LSC 6163/SER 5509-5511 lp: decca 2BB 104-106/417 1681 lp: london (usa) OSA 1395 cd: decca 417 1682
vienna 17-28 october 1978	vienna philharmonic vienna opera chorus armstrong ihloff lindenstrand szirmay cosotti bacquier stilwell	vhs video: decca 071 4033
berlin 6-8 march 1993	berlin philharmonic rundfunkchor serra norberg-schulz graham lipovsek canonici van dam nucci	cd: decca 440 6502

verdi **la forza del destino**

london	covent garden	cd: myto MCD 003.224
1 october	orchestra	
1962	and chorus	
	cavalli	
	veasey	
	bergonzi	
	shaw	
	ghiaurov	

la forza del destino, overture

london	london	78: decca X 298
29-31	philharmonic	78: london (usa) T 5659
august		lp: decca LK 4017/ACL 149
1949		lp: london (usa) LL 200/B 19047

also published on lp by everest

i lombardi, excerpts (gerusalem!; o signore del tetto natio!)

chicago	chicago so	cd: decca 430 2262
4-7	and chorus	
november		
1989		

macbeth, excerpts (tre volte miagola; patria oppressa!)

chicago	chicago so	cd: decca 430 2262
4-7	and chorus	
november		
1989		

i masnadieri, excerpt (le rube gli stupri)

chicago	chicago so	cd: decca 430 2262
4-7	and chorus	
november		
1989		

nabucco, excerpt (va pensiero!)

chicago	chicago so	cd: decca 430 2262/433 8222
4-7	and chorus	
november		
1989		

verdi **otello**

cologne april 1958	wdr orchestra and chorus watson hopf metternich *sung in german*	unpublished radio broadcast
london 30 june 1962	covent garden orchestra and chorus kabaiwanska del monaco gobbi	cd: nuova era NE 2357-2358
new york 23 march 1963	metropolitan opera orchestra and chorus tucci mccracken merrill	unpublished met broadcast
london may 1968	covent garden orchestra and chorus tarres cassilly taddei	unpublished radio broadcast *music performance research centre*
vienna 14-21 september 1977	vienna philharmonic vienna opera chorus m.price cossutta bacquier	lp: decca D102 D3 lp: london (usa) OSA 13130 cd: decca 440 0452/460 7562
chicago 8-12 april and new york 16-19 april 1991	chicago so and chorus kanawa pavarotti nucci	cd: decca 433 6692 *excerpts* cd: decca 440 8432
london 27 october 1992	covent garden orchestra and chorus kanawa domingo leiferkus	vhs video: castle CVI 1718 vhs video: kultur (usa) 1492 laserdisc: pioneer PLMC 00851

verdi **otello, excerpt (fuoco di gioia!)**
london	covent garden	lp: decca SET 392-393
22-23	orchestra	lp: london (usa) OSA 1276
february	and chorus	
1968	dobson	
	gobbi	
chicago	chicago so	cd: decca 430 2262
4-7	and chorus	
november 1989		

rigoletto
rome	rca italiana	lp: victor LM 7027/LMDS 7027/
17-27	orchestra	RE 5516-5517/SER 5516-5517
june	and chorus	cd: rca/bmg GD 86506
1963	moffo	*excerpts*
	elias	lp: victor LM 2837/LSC 2837/
	kraus	VCS 7092/RB 16029
	merrill	cd: rca/bmg 09026 608412
	flagello	
london	covent garden	unpublished radio broadcast
10 february	orchestra	*music performance research centre*
1964	and chorus	
	moffo	
	guy	
	cossutta	
	glossop	

simon boccanegra
milan	la scala	cd: decca 425 6282
12-22	orchestra	
december	and chorus	
1988	kanawa	
	aragall	
	nucci	
london	covent garden	vhs video: decca 071 4233
1992	orchestra	*also unpublished video recording of*
	and chorus	*rehearsal extracts*
	kanawa	
	sylvester	
	agache	
london	covent garden	unpublished radio broadcast
3 june	orchestra	*music performance research centre*
1997	and chorus	
	kanawa	
	giordani	
	agache	

verdi la traviata

london	covent garden	cd: decca 448 1192
november-	orchestra	vhs video: decca 071 4313
december	and chorus	dvd: decca 071 4312
1994	gheorghiu	*excerpts*
	lopardo	cd: decca 452 1942/458 2742

london	covent garden	unpublished radio broadcast
1 july	orchestra	*music performance research centre*
1995	and chorus	
	vaness	
	giordani	
	nucci	

la traviata, excerpt (libiamo ne' lieti calici!)

london	covent garden	unpublished radio broadcast
25 february	orchestra	*music performance research centre*
1990	and chorus	
	tomowa-sintov	
	davies	

la traviata, excerpts (noi siamo zingarelle; di madride no siam mattadori)

chicago	chicago so	cd: decca 430 2262
4-7	and chorus	
november		
1989		

la traviata, preludes to acts one and three

london	covent garden	lp: victor LM 2313/LSC 2313/RB 16172/
18-21	orchestra	SB 2058/VIC 1119/VICS 1119
june		lp: decca SPA 347
1958		lp: london (usa) CS 6753
		act one prelude
		cd: decca 460 9822

also two unpublished radio broadcasts of act one prelude with covent garden orchestra

il trovatore, excerpts (vedi le foschel; squilli echeggi)

chicago	chicago so	cd: decca 430 2262
4-7	and chorus	
november		
1989		

verdi **messa da requiem**

cologne 17 november 1958	wdr orchestra and chorus brouwenstijn dominguez zampieri zaccaria	lp: movimento musica 02.009 cd: globe GLO 5141
new york 28 march 1964	metropolitan opera orchestra and chorus price elias bergonzi siepi	unpublished met broadcast
vienna 18-28 october 1967	vienna philharmonic vienna opera chorus sutherland horne pavarotti talvela	lp: decca SET 374-375 lp: london (usa) OSA 1275 cd: decca 411 9442
chicago 1-2 june 1977	chicago so and chorus price baker lucchetti van dam	lp: victor RL 22476/ARL2-2476 cd: rca/bmg RD 82476/09026 614032 *excerpts* cd: rca/bmg GD 60206

messa da requiem, excerpt (sanctus)

chicago 4-7 november 1989	chicago so and chorus	cd: decca 430 2262

quattro pezzi sacri

chicago 23 may 1977	chicago so and chorus pickens	lp: decca SET 602 lp: london (usa) OS 26610 cd: decca 425 8442 *recording completed on 22 may 1978*

RICHARD WAGNER (1813-1883)

der fliegende holländer

chicago	chicago so	lp: decca D24 D3
18-22	and chorus	lp: london (usa) OSA 13119
may	martin	cd: decca 414 5512/430 4482
1976	kollo	*excerpts*
	krenn	lp: decca 411 9511
	bailey	lp: london (usa) CS 7078
	talvela	cd: decca 411 9512/417 7522/421 8652/ 430 4482/430 6352/440 0692/ 448 2502/460 9822/466 4672

der fliegende holländer, overture

vienna	vienna	lp: decca MET 227/SET 227/
11-13	philharmonic	SXL 6292/VIV 30
october		lp: london (usa) CM 9314/CS 6245/
1961		CS 6782
		cd: decca 433 4072/440 6062

london	covent garden	unpublished video recording
1964	orchestra	*rehearsal extract only*

chicago	chicago so	laserdisc: decca 071 1011
1-2		
june		
1976		

götterdämmerung

london	covent garden	unpublished radio broadcast
14 september	orchestra	
1963	and chorus	
	nilsson	
	collier	
	veasey	
	windgassen	
	stewart	
	frick	
	kraus	

wagner götterdämmerung/concluded

vienna
20 may–
6 june
1964
	vienna
	philharmonic
	vienna opera
	chorus
	nilsson
	watson
	ludwig
	windgassen
	fischer-dieskau
	frick
	neidlinger
		lp: decca MET 292-297/SET 292-297/
		   D100 D19/RING 1-22/414 1001/
		   414 1151
		lp: london (usa) A 4604/OSA 1604
		cd: decca 414 1002/414 1152/
		   455 5692/455 5552
		excerpts
		lp: decca LXT 6220/LXT 6261/SXL 6220/
		   SXL 6261/GRV 7/GRV 18/
		   GRV 24/417 1811
		lp: london (usa) OS 25991
		cd: decca 421 3132/440 4832/448 9332/
		   458 3982/460 6102
		rehearsal extracts
		vhs video: decca 071 0023/071 1533
		recording completed 26 october–24 november 1964

götterdämmerung, act three

london 6 september 1963	covent garden orchestra and chorus nilsson collier windgassen stewart frick	unpublished radio broadcast *promenade concert performance prior to new production of complete opera at covent garden (see entry above for 14 september 1963)*

götterdämmerung, siegfried's rhine journey

london 6 september 1963	covent garden orchestra	unpublished radio broadcast

götterdämmerung, funeral march and orchestral finale

vienna 11-15 october 1982	vienna philharmonic	lp: decca SXDL 7612 lp: london (usa) LDR 71112 cd: decca 410 1372/433 4072/440 6062

kose und –rosenlied/kinderkatechismus

vienna july 1969	members of vienna philharmonic wiener sängerknaben	lp: decca SET 406-408 lp: london (usa) RDNS 1 *it is not entirely clear whether solti actually conducted this musical example for the lp set "an introduction to the ring"*

wagner **lohengrin**

vienna 11-15 november 1985	vienna philharmonic vienna opera chorus norman randova domingo nimsgern sotin	lp: decca 421 0531 cd: decca 421 0532 *excerpts* cd: decca 421 8652/425 5302/430 7112/ 440 0692/460 6102/466 4672 *recording completed in december 1985 and* *june 1986*

die meistersinger von nürnberg

london february 1969	covent garden orchestra and chorus ruk-focic veasey thomas shirley h.hofmann ward evans	unpublished radio broadcast *music performance research centre*
vienna 15 september- 14 october 1975	vienna philharmonic vienna opera chorus bode hamari kollo dallapozza bailey nienstedt weikl	lp: decca D13 D5 lp: london (usa) OSA 1512 cd: decca 417 4972 *excerpts* lp: decca JB 142 cd: decca 466 4702
chicago 23-27 september 1995	chicago so and chorus mattila vermillion heppner lippert van dam pape opie	cd: decca 452 6062

wagner **die meistersinger von nürnberg, overture**
chicago 16-17 may 1972	chicago so	lp: decca SXL 6684/411 9511 lp: london (usa) CS 6800/CS 7078/CS 7252 cd: decca 411 9512/417 7522/430 4482/ 440 0692/460 9822
chicago 1-2 june 1976	chicago so	laserdisc: decca 071 1101
new york 13 june 1994	orchestra of the solti orchestral project	cd: decca 444 4582

parsifal
new york 28 march 1964	metropolitan opera orchestra thomas hines	unpublished met broadcast *act three scene one only*
vienna 3-17 december 1971	vienna philharmonic vienna opera chorus ludwig kollo fischer-dieskau hotter kelemen frick	lp: decca SET 550-554 lp: london (usa) OSA 1510 cd: decca 417 1432 *excerpts* lp: decca GRV 18 *recording completed in march and june 1972*

das rheingold

vienna
24 september-
8 october
1958
	vienna
	philharmonic
	flagstad
	svanholm
	kuen
	london
	neidlinger
		lp: decca LXT 5495-5497/SXL 2101-2103/
		    SET 382-384/D100 D19/RING 1-22/
		    414 1011/414 1001
		lp: london (usa) A 4340/OSA 1309
		cd: decca 414 1012/414 1002/
		    455 5552/455 5562
		excerpts
		45: decca CEP 632/SEC 5042
		lp: decca LXT 5586/SXL 2230
		lp: london (usa) CM 5335/OS 25126
		cd: decca 421 3132/448 9332/466 2612

london 16 september 1965	covent garden orchestra veasey, stolze, lanigan, ward, neidlinger	unpublished radio broadcast *music performance research centre*

wagner **das rheingold, entry of the gods into valhalla**
vienna	vienna	lp: decca SXDL 7612
11-15	philharmonic	lp: london (usa) LDR 71112
october		cd: decca 410 1372/433 4072/
1982		440 6062/466 4672

rienzi, overture
vienna	vienna	lp: decca MET 227/SET 227/
11-13	philharmonic	SXL 6292/VIV 30
october		lp: london (usa) CM 9314/CS 6245/
1961		CS 6782
		cd: decca 433 4072/440 6062

siegfried
vienna	vienna	lp: decca MET 242-245/SET 242-246/
8-18	philharmonic	D100 D19/RING 1-22/414 1001/
may	nilsson	414 1101
1962	sutherland	lp: london (usa) A 4508/OSA 1508
	höffgen	cd: decca 414 1002/414 1102/
	windgassen	455 5642/455 5552
	stolze	*excerpts*
	hotter	lp: decca LXT 6142/SXL 6142
	neidlinger	lp: london (usa) OS 25898
		cd: decca 448 9332/458 3982/
		460 6102/466 2612
		recording completed 22 october-5 november 1962

siegfried, forest murmurs
vienna	vienna	lp: decca SXDL 7612
11-15	philharmonic	lp: london (usa) LDR 71112
october		cd: decca 410 1372/433 4072/440 6062
1982		

siegfried idyll
vienna	vienna	lp: decca MET 323-324/SET 323-324
20-28	philharmonic	lp: london (usa) CMA 7216/OSA 2216/
october		CS 7252
1965		cd: decca 460 3112

wagner **tannhäuser**

new york	metropolitan	unpublished met broadcast
17 december	opera orchestra	*excerpts*
1960	and chorus	lp: melodram MEL 085
	rysanek	
	dalis	
	allen	
	hopf	
	prey	
	hines	
	rothmüller	
vienna	vienna	lp: decca SET 506-509
3-21	philharmonic	lp: london (usa) OSA 1438
october	vienna opera	cd: decca 414 5812
1970	chorus	*excerpts*
	dernesch	lp: decca SET 556/GRV 18
	ludwig	lp: london (usa) OS 26299
	kollo	cd: decca 440 0692/460 6102
	hollweg	
	braun	
	sotin	

tannhäuser, excerpt (dich teure halle!)

chicago	chicago so	cd: chicago symphony orchestra CD 9010
29 april	price	
1980		

tannhäuser, overture

london	covent garden	unpublished radio broadcast
undated	orchestra	
chicago	chicago so	laserdisc: decca 071 1011
1-2		
june		
1976		
chicago	chicago so	lp: decca SXL 6856/411 9511
23 may		lp: london (usa) CS 7078
1977		cd: decca 411 9512/430 4482/466 4672

tannhäuser, overture and venusberg music

vienna	vienna	lp: decca MET 227/SET 227/
11-13	philharmonic	SXL 6292/VIV 30
october	wiener	lp: london (usa) CM 9314/CS 6245/
1961	singverein	CS 6782
		cd: decca 433 4072/440 6062

wagner **tristan und isolde**

vienna
2-30
september
1960
	vienna
	philharmonic
	vienna opera
	chorus
	nilsson
	resnik
	uhl
	krause
	van mill
		lp: decca MET 204-208/SET 204-208/
		    D41 D5
		lp: london (usa) A 4506/OSA 1502
		cd: decca 430 2342
		excerpts
		lp: decca LXT 6178/SXL 6178/SPA 317
		lp: london (usa) 7037/CS 7252/OS 25938
		lp: eterna 820 634
		cd: decca 430 1362/433 4072/440 0692/
		    448 8812/458 3142/458 3982/460 6102
		original lp sets also included rehearsal extracts

new york 23 february 1963	metropolitan opera orchestra and chorus nilsson dalis liebl cassel hines	unpublished met broadcast
london 3 july 1971	covent garden orchestra and chorus nilsson veasey thomas mcintyre ward	unpublished radio broadcast *music performance research centre*

tristan und isolde, prelude and liebestod

london 6 september 1963	covent garden orchestra nilsson	unpublished radio broadcast

wagner **tristan und isolde, prelude and liebestod in orchestral version**
london covent garden unpublished radio broadcast
undated orchestra

chicago chicago so vhs video: decca 071 1013
1-2
june
1976

chicago chicago so lp: decca SXL 6856/411 9511
18-23 lp: london (usa) CS 7078
may cd: decca 411 9512/417 7522/430 4482/
1977   430 6352/440 7292

die walküre
vienna vienna lp: decca MET 312-316/SET 312-316/
29 october- philharmonic   D100 D19/RING 1-22/414 1001/
19 november nilsson   414 1051
1965 crespin lp: london (usa) OSA 1509
    ludwig cd: decca 414 1002/414 1052/
    king   455 5592/455 5552
    hotter *excerpts*
    frick lp: decca SET 390/GRV 18
    lp: london (usa) OS 26085
    cd: decca 421 8872/448 9332/
        460 6102/466 2612

die walküre, act one
munich bavarian lp: orfeo S120 842I
7 may state cd: orfeo C019 991Z
1947 orchestra
    schech
    völker
    dalberg

die walküre, act three
vienna vienna lp: decca LXT 5389-5390/SXL 2031-2032/
13-28 philharmonic   GOM 577-578/GOS 577-578
may flagstad lp: london (usa) A 4225/OSA 1203
1957 schech cd: decca 425 9862/448 5752/467 1242
    edelmann *excerpts*
    45: decca CEP 598/SEC 5020
    cd: decca 440 3502
    excerpts also published on a stereo demonstration lp

wagner **die walküre, excerpt (siegmund sieh auf mich!)**

vienna	vienna	lp: decca LXT 5389-5390/SXL 2031-2032/
13-28	philharmonic	GOM 577-578/GOS 577-578
may	flagstad	lp: london (usa) A 4225/OSA 1203
1957	svanholm	cd: decca 440 4952/440 4902

die walküre, ride of the valkyries

london	covent garden	unpublished radio broadcast
undated	orchestra	
vienna	vienna	lp: decca SXDL 7612
11-15	philharmonic	lp: london (usa) LDR 71112
october		cd: decca 410 1372/433 4072/
1982		440 0692/440 6062

die walküre, magic fire music

vienna	vienna	lp: decca SXDL 7612
11-15	philharmonic	lp: london (usa) LDR 71112
october		cd: decca 410 1372/433 4072/440 6062
1982		

der ring des nibelungen: in addition to the recordings of the individual music dramas listed above, unpublished radio broadcasts of complete cycles conducted by solti survive from covent garden (1964-1968) and from the bayreuth festival (1983)

WILLIAM WALTON (1902-1983)

belshazzar's feast
london	london	lp: decca SET 618
2-4	philharmonic	lp: london (usa) OS 26525
march	alldis choir	lp: london philharmonic orchestra LPJ 50
1977	luxon	cd: decca 425 1542/440 3242

coronation te deum
london	london	lp: decca SET 618
2-4	philharmonic	lp: london (usa) OS 26525
march	alldis and	cd: decca 425 1542/436 4032/440 3242
1977	cathedral	
	choirs	

portsmouth point, overture
cologne	wdr orchestra	unpublished radio broadcast
21 january		
1952		

CARL MARIA VON WEBER (1786-1826)

oberon, overture
chicago	chicago so	lp: decca SXL 6830
9 november		lp: london (usa) CS 7050
1973		cd: decca 460 9822
		also private lp issue by chicago symphony orchestra

LEO WEINER (1885-1960)

serenade
budapest	budapest	cd: decca 458 9292
vienna	festival	
1997	orchestra	

prinz csongor und die kobolde, introduction and scherzo
chicago	chicago so	cd: decca 443 4442
november		
1993		
vienna	vienna	vhs video: decca 071 1843
april		
1995		

MISCELLANEOUS

british national anthem, arranged by elgar
london	london	45: decca F 13713
7-18	philharmonic	lp: decca SXL 6848
february		lp: london (usa) CS 7072
1977		cd: decca 440 3172
		recording completed in march-april 1977

bear down chicago; the star spangled banner
chicago	chicago so	lp: decca 417 3971
27 january		
1987		

sixtieth birthday gala for queen elizabeth II
london	covent garden	unpublished video recording
21 april	orchestra	*music performance research centre*
1988	norman	
	domingo	
	carreras	
	solti and	
	downes,	
	conductors	

orchestra!: music for the channel four tv series
19-28	schleswig-	cd: decca 430 8382
june	holstein	vhs video: decca 071 1293/071 1303/
1990	festival	071 1313
	orchestra	
	solti, piano	
	and conductor	
	moore, piano	

miscellaneous/concluded
immortal beloved: soundtrack to the film
london　　　　london so　　　　cd: sony SK 66301
undated　　　　london voices
　　　　　　　　fleming
　　　　　　　　murray
　　　　　　　　cole
　　　　　　　　terfel
　　　　　　　　kremer
　　　　　　　　frank
　　　　　　　　ma
　　　　　　　　ax

interview with john culshaw on the recording of tristan und isolde
1960　　　　　　　　　　　　lp: decca MET 204-208/SET 204-208
　　　　　　　　　　　　　　lp: london (usa) A 4506/OSA 1502

interview with william mann on recording the beethoven symphonies
1974　　　　　　　　　　　　lp: decca 11BB 188-196
　　　　　　　　　　　　　　lp: london (usa) CSP 9

documentary on the making of wagner's ring
1964　　　　　　　　　　　　vhs video: decca 071 0023/071 1533

the making of a maestro: documentary by peter maniura
1997　　　　　　　　　　　　unpublished video recording

details of a further tv documentary entitled solti revisited, published on video by rm arts, could not be verified

1999: 978-1-901395-97-6: The Furtwaengler Sound Sixth Edition: Discography and Concert Listing.
1999: 978-1-901395-98-3: The Great Dictators: 3 Discographies: Evgeny Mravinsky, Artur Rodzinski, Sergiu Celibidache.
1999: 978-1-901395-99-0: Sviatoslav Richter: Pianist of the Century: Discography.
2000: 978-1-901395-04-4: Philharmonic Autocrat 1: Discography of: Herbert Von Karajan [Third Edition].
2000: 978-1-901395-05-1: Wiener Philharmoniker 1 - Vienna Philharmonic and Vienna State Opera Orchestras: Discography Part 1 1905-1954.
2000: 978-1-901395-06-8: Wiener Philharmoniker 2 - Vienna Philharmonic and Vienna State Opera Orchestras: Discography Part 2 1954-1989.
2001: 978-1-901395-07-5: Gramophone Stalwarts: 3 Separate Discographies: Bruno Walter, Erich Leinsdorf, Georg Solti.
2001: 978-1-901395-08-2: Singers of the Third Reich: 5 Discographies: Helge Roswaenge, Tiana Lemnitz, Franz Voelker, Maria Mueller, Max Lorenz.
2001: 978-1-901395-09-9: Philharmonic Autocrat 2: Concert Register of Herbert Von Karajan Second Edition.
2002: 978-1-901395-10-5: Sächsische Staatskapelle Dresden: Complete Discography.
2002: 978-1-901395-11-2: Carlo Maria Giulini: Discography and Concert Register.
2002: 978-1-901395-12-9: Pianists For The Connoisseur: 6 Discographies: Arturo Benedetti Michelangeli, Alfred Cortot, Alexis Weissenberg, Clifford Curzon, Solomon, Elly Ney.
2003: 978-1-901395-14-3: Singers on the Yellow Label: 7 Discographies: Maria Stader, Elfriede Troetschel, Annelies Kupper, Wolfgang Windgassen, Ernst Haefliger, Josef Greindl, Kim Borg.
2003: 978-1-901395-15-0: A Gallic Trio: 3 Discographies: Charles Muench, Paul Paray, Pierre Monteux.
2004: 978-1-901395-16-7: Antal Dorati 1906-1988: Discography and Concert Register.
2004: 978-1-901395-17-4: Columbia 33CX Label Discography.
2004: 978-1-901395-18-1: Great Violinists: 3 Discographies: David Oistrakh, Wolfgang Schneiderhan, Arthur Grumiaux.
2006: 978-1-901395-19-8: Leopold Stokowski: Second Edition of the Discography.
2006: 978-1-901395-20-4: Wagner Im Festspielhaus: Discography of the Bayreuth Festival.
2006: 978-1-901395-21-1: Her Master's Voice: Concert Register and Discography of Dame Elisabeth Schwarzkopf [Third Edition].
2007: 978-1-901395-22-8: Hans Knappertsbusch: Kna: Concert Register and Discography of Hans Knappertsbusch, 1888-1965. Second Edition.
2008: 978-1-901395-23-5: Philips Minigroove: Second Extended Version of the European Discography.
2009: 978-1-901395--24-2: American Classics: The Discographies of Leonard Bernstein and Eugene Ormandy.

Discography by Stephen J. Pettitt, edited by John Hunt:
1987: 978-1-906857-16-5: Philharmonia Orchestra: Complete Discography 1945-1987

Available from: Travis & Emery at 17 Cecil Court, London, UK. (+44) 20 7 240 2129. email on sales@travis-and-emery.com .

© Travis & Emery 2009

Discographies by Travis & Emery:

Discographies by John Hunt.

1987: 978-1-906857-14-1: From Adam to Webern: the Recordings of von Karajan.

1991: 978-0-951026-83-0: 3 Italian Conductors and 7 Viennese Sopranos: 10 Discographies: Arturo Toscanini, Guido Cantelli, Carlo Maria Giulini, Elisabeth Schwarzkopf, Irmgard Seefried, Elisabeth Gruemmer, Sena Jurinac, Hilde Gueden, Lisa Della Casa, Rita Streich.

1992: 978-0-951026-85-4: Mid-Century Conductors and More Viennese Singers: 10 Discographies: Karl Boehm, Victor De Sabata, Hans Knappertsbusch, Tullio Serafin, Clemens Krauss, Anton Dermota, Leonie Rysanek, Eberhard Waechter, Maria Reining, Erich Kunz.

1993: 978-0-951026-87-8: More 20th Century Conductors: 7 Discographies: Eugen Jochum, Ferenc Fricsay, Carl Schuricht, Felix Weingartner, Josef Krips, Otto Klemperer, Erich Kleiber.

1994: 978-0-951026-88-5: Giants of the Keyboard: 6 Discographies: Wilhelm Kempff, Walter Gieseking, Edwin Fischer, Clara Haskil, Wilhelm Backhaus, Artur Schnabel.

1994: 978-0-951026-89-2: Six Wagnerian Sopranos: 6 Discographies: Frieda Leider, Kirsten Flagstad, Astrid Varnay, Martha Moedl, Birgit Nilsson, Gwyneth Jones.

1995: 978-0-952582-70-0: Musical Knights: 6 Discographies: Henry Wood, Thomas Beecham, Adrian Boult, John Barbirolli, Reginald Goodall, Malcolm Sargent.

1995: 978-0-952582-71-7: A Notable Quartet: 4 Discographies: Gundula Janowitz, Christa Ludwig, Nicolai Gedda, Dietrich Fischer-Dieskau.

1996: 978-0-952582-72-4: The Post-War German Tradition: 5 Discographies: Rudolf Kempe, Joseph Keilberth, Wolfgang Sawallisch, Rafael Kubelik, Andre Cluytens.

1996: 978-0-952582-73-1: Teachers and Pupils: 7 Discographies: Elisabeth Schwarzkopf, Maria Ivoguen, Maria Cebotari, Meta Seinemeyer, Ljuba Welitsch, Rita Streich, Erna Berger.

1996: 978-0-952582-77-9: Tenors in a Lyric Tradition: 3 Discographies: Peter Anders, Walther Ludwig, Fritz Wunderlich.

1997: 978-0-952582-78-6: The Lyric Baritone: 5 Discographies: Hans Reinmar, Gerhard Huesch, Josef Metternich, Hermann Uhde, Eberhard Waechter.

1997: 978-0-952582-79-3: Hungarians in Exile: 3 Discographies: Fritz Reiner, Antal Dorati, George Szell.

1997: 978-1-901395-00-6: The Art of the Diva: 3 Discographies: Claudia Muzio, Maria Callas, Magda Olivero.

1997: 978-1-901395-01-3: Metropolitan Sopranos: 4 Discographies: Rosa Ponselle, Eleanor Steber, Zinka Milanov, Leontyne Price.

1997: 978-1-901395-02-0: Back From The Shadows: 4 Discographies: Willem Mengelberg, Dimitri Mitropoulos, Hermann Abendroth, Eduard Van Beinum.

1997: 978-1-901395-03-7: More Musical Knights: 4 Discographies: Hamilton Harty, Charles Mackerras, Simon Rattle, John Pritchard.

1998: 978-1-901395-94-5: Conductors On The Yellow Label: 8 Discographies: Fritz Lehmann, Ferdinand Leitner, Ferenc Fricsay, Eugen Jochum, Leopold Ludwig, Artur Rother, Franz Konwitschny, Igor Markevitch.

1998: 978-1-901395-95-2: More Giants of the Keyboard: 5 Discographies: Claudio Arrau, Gyorgy Cziffra, Vladimir Horowitz, Dinu Lipatti, Artur Rubinstein.

1998: 978-1-901395-96-9: Mezzo and Contraltos: 5 Discographies: Janet Baker, Margarete Klose, Kathleen Ferrier, Giulietta Simionato, Elisabeth Hoengen.

Music and Books published by Travis & Emery Music Bookshop:

Mellers, Wilfrid: François Couperin and the French Classical Tradition
Mellers, Wilfrid: Harmonious Meeting
Mellers, Wilfrid: Le Jardin Retrouvé, The Music of Frederic Mompou
Mellers, Wilfrid: Music and Society, England and the European Tradition
Mellers, Wilfrid: Music in a New Found Land: ... ... American Music
Mellers, Wilfrid: Romanticism and the Twentieth Century (from 1800)
Mellers, Wilfrid: The Masks of Orpheus: ...... the Story of European Music.
Mellers, Wilfrid: The Sonata Principle (from c. 1750)
Mellers, Wilfrid: Vaughan Williams and the Vision of Albion
Panchianio, Cattuffio: Rutzvanscad Il Giovine (1737)
Pearce, Charles: Sims Reeves, Fifty Years of Music in England.
Pettitt, Stephen: Philharmonia Orchestra: Complete Discography (1987)
Playford, John: An Introduction to the Skill of Musick (1674)
Purcell, Henry et al: Harmonia Sacra ... The First Book, (1726)
Purcell, Henry et al: Harmonia Sacra ... Book II (1726)
Quantz, Johann: Versuch einer Anweisung die Flöte traversiere zu spielen.
Rameau, Jean-Philippe: Code de Musique Pratique, ou Methodes (1760)
Rastall, Richard: The Notation of Western Music.
Rimbault, Edward: The Pianoforte, Its Origins, Progress, and Construction.
Rousseau, Jean Jacques: Dictionnaire de Musique
Rubinstein, Anton : Guide to the proper use of the Pianoforte Pedals.
Sainsbury, John S.: Dictionary of Musicians. Vol. 1. (1825). 2 vols.
Serré de Rieux, Jean de : Les dons des Enfans de Latone
Simpson, Christopher: A Compendium of Practical Musick in Five Parts
Spohr, Louis: Autobiography
Spohr, Louis: Grand Violin School
Tans'ur, William: A New Musical Grammar; or The Harmonical Spectator
Terry, Charles Sanford: John Christian Bach (Johann Christian Bach) (1929)
Terry, Charles Sanford: J.S. Bach's Original Hymn-Tunes for Congregational Use
Terry, Charles Sanford: Four-Part Chorals of J.S. Bach. (German & English)
Terry, Charles Sanford: Joh. Seb. Bach, Cantata Texts, Sacred and Secular.
Terry, Charles Sanford: The Origins of the Family of Bach Musicians.
Tosi, Pierfrancesco: Opinioni de' Cantori Antichi, e Moderni (1723)
Van der Straeten, Edmund: History of the Violoncello, The Viol da Gamba ...
Van der Straeten, Edmund: History of the Violin, Its Ancestors... (2 vols.)
Waltern: Musikalisches Lexicon
Walther, J. G.: Musicalisches Lexikon ober Musicalische Bibliothec

Travis & Emery Music Bookshop
17 Cecil Court, London, WC2N 4EZ, United Kingdom.
Tel. (+44) 20 7240 2129

© Travis & Emery 2009

Music and Books published by Travis & Emery Music Bookshop:

Anon.: Hymnarium Sarisburiense, cum Rubricis et Notis Musicis.
Agricola, Johann Friedrich from Tosi: Anleitung zur Singkunst.
Bach, C.P.E.: edited W. Emery: Nekrolog or Obituary Notice of J.S. Bach.
Bateson, Naomi Judith: Alcock of Salisbury
Bathe, William: A Briefe Introduction to the Skill of Song (c.1587)
Bax, Arnold: Symphony #5, Arranged for Piano Four Hands by Walter Emery
Burney, Charles: The Present State of Music in France and Italy (1771)
Burney, Charles: The Present State of Music in Germany, Netherlands... (1773)
Burney, Charles: An Account of the Musical Performances ... Handel (1784)
Burney, Karl: Nachricht von Georg Friedrich Handel's Lebensumstanden (1784)
Burns, Robert: The Caledonian Musical Museum ... Best Scotch Songs (1810)
Cobbett, W.W.: Cobbett's Cyclopedic Survey of Chamber Music. (2 vols.)
Corrette, Michel: Le Maitre de Clavecin (1753)
Crimp, Bryan: Dear Mr. Rosenthal ... Dear Mr. Gaisberg ...
Crimp, Bryan: Solo: The Biography of Solomon
d'Indy, Vincent: Beethoven: Biographie Critique (in French, 1911)
d'Indy, Vincent: Beethoven: A Critical Biography (in English, 1912)
d'Indy, Vincent: César Franck (in French, 1910)
Fischhof, Joseph: Versuch einer Geschichte des Clavierbaues (1853).
Frescobaldi, Girolamo: D'Arie Musicali per Cantarsi. Primo & Secondo Libro
Geminiani, Francesco: The Art of Playing the Violin (1751)
Handel; Purcell; Boyce et al: Calliope or English Harmony: Vol. First. (1746)
Häuser: Musikalisches Lexikon. 2 vols in one.
Hawkins, John: General History of the Science & Practice of Music (5 vols. 1776)
Herbert-Caesari, Edgar: The Science and Sensations of Vocal Tone
Herbert-Caesari, Edgar: Vocal Truth
Hopkins and Rimboult: The Organ. Its History and Construction.
Hunt, John: Adam to Webern: the recordings of von Karajan
Hunt, John: several discographies – see separate list.
Isaacs, Lewis: Hänsel and Gretel. A Guide to Humperdinck's Opera.
Isaacs, Lewis: Königskinder (Royal Children) A Guide to Humperdinck's Opera.
Kastner: Manuel Général de Musique Militaire
Lacassagne, M. l'Abbé Joseph : Traité Général des élémens du Chant.
Lascelles (née Catley), Anne: The Life of Miss Anne Catley.
Mainwaring, John: Memoirs of the Life of the Late George Frederic Handel
Malcolm, Alexander: A Treaty of Music: Speculative, Practical and Historical
Marx, Adolph Bernhard: Die Kunst des Gesanges, Theoretisch-Practisch (1826)
May, Florence: The Life of Brahms (2nd edition)
May, Florence: The Girlhood Of Clara Schumann: Clara Wieck And Her Time.
Mellers, Wilfrid: Angels of the Night: Popular Female Singers of Our Time
Mellers, Wilfrid: Bach and the Dance of God
Mellers, Wilfrid: Beethoven and the Voice of God
Mellers, Wilfrid: Caliban Reborn - Renewal in Twentieth Century Music

www.ingramcontent.com/pod-product-compliance
Lightning Source LLC
Chambersburg PA
CBHW052049230426
43671CB00011B/1848